Dancing to a
Different Rhythm

Dancing to a
Different Rhythm

Zarina Maharaj

ZEBRA

Published by Zebra Press
an imprint of Struik Publishers
(a division of New Holland Publishing (South Africa) (Pty) Ltd)
PO Box 1144, Cape Town, 8000
New Holland Publishing is a member of Johnnic Communications Ltd

www.zebrapress.co.za

First published 2006

1 3 5 7 9 10 8 6 4 2

Publication © Zebra Press 2006
Text © Zarina Maharaj 2006

Cover photographs © Gallo Images/www.gettyimages.com/SambaPhoto

PUBLISHING MANAGER: Marlene Fryer
MANAGING EDITOR: Robert Plummer
EDITOR: Ronel Richter-Herbert
COVER AND TEXT DESIGNER: Natascha Adendorff-Olivier
TYPESETTER: Monique van den Berg
INDEXER: Robert Plummer
PRODUCTION MANAGER: Valerie Kömmer

Set in 11.5 pt on 16 pt Adobe Caslon

Reproduction by Hirt & Carter (Cape) (Pty) Ltd
Printed and bound by Paarl Print, Oosterland Street, Paarl, South Africa

ISBN 1-77007-108-3

For Joey and Milou

'*You, the children, were the foot soldiers in our fight for freedom.*'
President Nelson Mandela, 1998

Thank you for your courage

Contents

PART I

The Last Stepping Stone

CHAPTER I

Not *when* ... but *if* ...

SUSSEX

I had just finished packing our suitcases after selling off the last bits of furniture and the kids had finally fallen off to sleep. I was about to call it a day when, at half past twelve on 25 July 1990, the phone pierced the silence of the Sussex night. Nervously I answered, thinking, no one rings me at this time of the night.

'Hi, Zarina,' a voice said at the other end. 'This is Valli Moosa calling from South Africa. We've never met, but we know of each other through Mac ...'

'Is Mac okay?' I interrupted anxiously, almost rudely, as a shudder ran down my spine. Why would someone so senior in the South African liberation movement call me out of the blue at this time of night, just as the kids and I were about to board a flight to South Africa the following evening?

'Is there anything wrong, Valli?' I asked, still not giving him a chance to talk, afraid to hear why he'd called on the eve of our long-awaited return home. 'Mac must have told you how desperate we are to be reunited after all this time living apart. Will he be at the airport day after tomorrow?'

'No, I'm afraid not,' Valli said. 'Mac was ambushed on his way to my house this evening by the Special Branch police. He's in jail again. I don't think you and the kids should fly out tomorrow. We have no idea when he'll be released.'

Listening to his voice quivering with emotion made me feel even more jittery, even as relief that Mac was still alive flooded through me. There had always been the possibility that his work in the underground struggle in South Africa would be the end of him. We had often discussed this possibility with Oliver Tambo, the president of the African National Congress, in the months prior to Mac's departure from Zambia in 1988. It was because of these discussions that 'OR' – or 'Chief', as he was affectionately called by those who worked with him – had written us a note in which he thanked us 'for who and what you are to us all'. I still drew strength from his words, and kept the framed note on my desk.

'How long will Mac be in, Valli?' I asked, as relief gave way to new uncertainties.

'I don't know,' Valli replied. 'But no doubt we'll know soon.'

I asked Valli how they could have arrested Mac when he'd been granted indemnity from prosecution for political offences committed before 8 October 1990, and when the Groote Schuur negotiations for a peaceful end to apartheid had already started between the ANC and the government.

'Mac should have gone into hiding when Gebuza and Pravin and some of the others were arrested two weeks ago,' I said, puzzled. 'He surely must have known he would be next?'

'I don't know,' Valli said patiently. 'He might have been clearing away incriminating evidence.'

Sure. Mac would rather die than give in to the enemy. Once before, while in detention at the Security Branch head office in Johannesburg, they had tortured him very badly when he wouldn't talk. Due to the injuries to his neck, his right arm was paralysed for three years of his subsequent twelve-year imprisonment on Robben Island. I trembled, trying to block any thoughts of what they might do to him now.

'We should never have trusted those apartheid brutes,' I said to Valli. 'What gall to arrest Mac when no date has been agreed on yet to cease the armed struggle. And now we can't go home! What do I tell the children? That they won't see their dad for another two years? That we were simply not meant to be together as a family?'

In an attempt to deal with the shock of the news, I began talking uncontrollably and without pause – and Valli let me. I told him that, no matter what, I would be on the next evening's flight to South Africa. At least we'd get to see Mac in prison. In any case, the house I had been occupying in Brighton had already been rented to someone else; I had just sold my car and furniture, taken both the children out of school and withdrawn from my studies at Sussex University. We had nowhere to stay and I had no desire to live in exile for another moment, not even for the essential treatment of the injuries I had sustained in a car accident in Lusaka, Zambia. (The UN had sent me to England for medical care in the hope that I would eventually return to work for them in Lusaka.)

And I just would not be able to cope with Milou and Joey's disappointment. They were so excited about being with their dad again, and couldn't wait to enjoy his undivided attention and listen to his jokes. Just being reminded of what he looked like had made their expectations soar in the last month.

'Mac's been arrested under the Internal Security Act,' Valli almost whispered. 'You know that this allows for indefinite detention, incommunicado, without trial, access to lawyers, medical care, friends or family. I'm really very sorry to have to tell you this, Zarina.'

This was a knockout blow. Indefinite detention and not even a chance of visiting him in prison – after all this time!

Sensing my despair, Valli continued. 'If you've been at all involved in Mac's underground work, you are at risk of imprisonment too – and how would that help to reunite the family? Are you there?' he prodded, getting no response from me.

The chill down my spine grew icier. What if they knew about the huge quantities of RPGs, hand grenades, AK47s, Makarovs and other military hardware Mac had been requesting in his communications – which I had sometimes had to decode and deliver to OR and Joe Slovo, or JS, chairman of the South African Communist Party, through Ivan Pillay, chief administrator of Operation Vula? Would the cops have discovered my collaboration, and that I was the 'Gemma' in the communications? The safe houses, documents and now fingerprints ... Would Mac have managed to clear all this evidence away, and what if they found it?

It was suddenly obvious that the children and I could not board our flight the next evening. I was too upset to carry on talking.

'I'll phone you when I've had a chance to think, Valli,' I said. 'I must go now. Thanks for all your time.'

Valli left me his phone number and a warm offer to help if he could.

As I put the phone down, my throat ached. Tears blurred my vision and the room began to reel. Mac was alive, but how badly were they torturing him this time? What do I tell the children? I wondered whether OR was well enough to have learnt of Mac's arrest. Mac was under OR's direct command, so he would get him out quickly, I consoled myself.

Following Mac's illegal entry into South Africa, OR had suffered a serious stroke in Lusaka. He was flown to London as an emergency case, where he remained critically ill for months. OR and JS had planned Operation Vulindlela (Open the Road) in the mid-eighties, at the height of apartheid repression, when the ANC leadership inside the country were either imprisoned, banned, in hiding or dead. They saw Vula, as it became known, as an opportunity to create the conditions in which the exiled ANC leadership could be resettled inside South Africa. This was a crucial new step in advancing the struggle. OR would be the overall commander, with JS as his deputy. OR had chosen Mac to enter South Africa illegally and head up the operation as its internal commander. Right from the outset, I fully supported Mac's appointment, as I saw it as our duty.

From the beginning, both OR and JS were deeply involved in Mac's preparations for entering and surviving inside the country, as they were with Gebuza's (Siphiwe Nyanda, later to become chief of staff of the

South African National Defence Force in democratic South Africa), whom Mac had proposed as his deputy commander. I was involved in helping Tim Jenkin, who had escaped from Pretoria Central Prison with Alex Moumbaris and Stephen Lee in the late seventies, to develop the underground communications system, training Gebuza and other Vula operatives in its use. I also operated the system from the Lusaka end in the initial stages. My full-time job with the UN carried diplomatic status, which allowed us to live in an area that provided cover for Mac's work.

Once I'd put the phone down, I kept telling myself that, even if OR was still too ill to intervene to get Mac released, JS was involved in the negotiations for a peaceful settlement. He'd make sure, with the help of the ANC, that nothing bad happened to Mac.

I'd lived with fears and uncertainties for Mac's life and our future for a long time. Yet what helped and sustained me through the difficult moments was the knowledge that we were living out our commitment in a way that, for me, could not have been more meaningful. I felt a deep sense of fulfilment acting out my beliefs, despite the dangers and the risks, and perhaps because of them. In the difficult times, it gave me strength to know that I stood alongside Mac in the front-line trenches in the fight against apartheid.

'Our beliefs, our commitment to whatever the struggle demands of us, become personal – intensely – because in concrete terms we seek to build a liveable life for the Joeys and Milous. Would that the soothsayer at Fort Vic was right about the long life ahead of you and me ... How glorious it would be if we could [live] through this to bask in the serenity of Milou and Joey in their thirties! How even more glorious it would be [if] we had before then carved a society that grants us all a liveable life!'

Mac had written this goodbye letter to me in Moscow while completing his final preparations to enter South Africa illegally. These preparations were meant to minimise his chances of being caught in the underground by the apartheid regime's powerful security apparatus. If caught, he might not survive.

A loneliness that had been haunting me was unleashed by the night's chilling phone call. It suddenly seemed to engulf my whole being. Political widowhood constantly threatened by actual widowhood was bad enough. But not being able to share my insecurities, anxieties and fears with my friends and comrades – I had to pretend to the children too – had made this a desolate life at times. I couldn't even show anyone Mac's letter, as they would know from the contents that he was not in a Moscow hospital, ill with a kidney disease, as his legend had everyone believe.

Yet I also felt fortified by the depth of his love for us. 'When I met you … I had reconciled myself to living with a void in my emotions. As for children, a family, any fleeting thoughts had long passed out of my mind when I went to prison. Then there was you. And fullness in life became a flood. By the time we had Milou and Joey I gloried in the three of you: everything "familoid" in me gushed out – something I never knew I had in me … The pain of missing you through physical separation always lives in me. But at this moment the intensity of the pain sears my heart and mind. It is a pain born out of the joy of living, because you give me strength … it is pain born of the passion of my love for you …'

I couldn't share even this with friends or comrades. Anything that could alert anyone to Vula was under wraps.

When Mac later legally re-entered South Africa under an indemnity from prosecution granted to all ANC leaders following Nelson Mandela's release from prison, I couldn't tell anyone that he had actually been underground in the country for some time and not in Moscow. For even then the South African police were not supposed to know that he had been in South Africa at all. No one was to find out that I knew his illness had been faked, or that I had conspired to keep the police off his trail in South Africa.

In February 1989, with Mac already operating from inside South Africa, OR and JS arranged that I 'visit' him at a hospital in Yalta so that I would be able to describe the place if the need ever arose. Except for a handful of people, no one had a clue that I was part of the communications team of Vula.

Sworn to secrecy, I could not draw on the support that my friends and comrades in Brighton and London would readily have given me if they'd known what I was going through. To them, my difficulties seemed typical of a single parent with an absent, sick husband. Of course they helped me when they could in this regard. But this void was exacerbated by the silence and pretence that I always had to maintain, whether I was relaxing with my Sussex friends, or in discussion groups with comrades or my fellow students, or during university outings, in single-parent groups, at school functions, children's parties, or out in the wonderful English countryside.

But now I would have to tell the children why we wouldn't be boarding our flight home. This would be the first time they would hear the truth about Mac's situation since he left home in Lusaka to go underground. I wondered whether I should tell them the truth, or whether I should make up some story to soften the blow. I decided to leave making a decision until the morning, when my head would be clearer. Then I'd also think about finding us new accommodation.

I made my way to bed at 4 a.m., checking on the children in their bunks in the tiny bedroom next to my mine. Joey, the five-year-old in the lower bunk, had kicked her bedding off as usual. I covered her and, as I stooped to kiss her, noticed how much she resembled her namesake, my mother Jo. She opened her eyes, smiled happily and murmured something about the old zebra tracksuit – a favourite of her dad's – that she would travel to South Africa in. My panic grew about telling them that we would not be going home after all. Cancelling a movie or some other much-anticipated outing with a child is usually disappointing enough for them. What about a flight home to meet your long-absent father? Using the nearby footstool, I reached up to kiss Milou, the eight-year-old. To my surprise, he was sucking his thumb, something he'd stopped doing when he was three. I was too exhausted and upset to give it much thought. I cuddled him, tucked him in and switched off the light.

At 6 a.m. the next morning, the shrill ring of the phone woke us all up. I rushed to the lounge to take the call, and noticed how stark and soulless the place had become without the Makonde carving, Malangatana drawings and Ben Macala painting which so nurtured my being, lifted my spirits and nourished my South African roots in this distant land. Sealed in boxes with other such pieces, and now airfreighted back to South Africa, it was as if a radiant life force had been extinguished from this terraced house in suburban Sussex. How much more cold and alien England already felt again!

'This is John Carlin from the *Sunday Independent* newspaper in South Africa,' the caller introduced himself. 'Mac was arrested here yesterday. He was the internal commander of Operation Vula, which had been setting up underground structures countrywide for the past two years in preparation for a military uprising ... Can you comment on that and on his arrest?'

This question really threw me. I was supposed to think Mac had been dying in Moscow, that he was now recovering and that, like other ANC leaders, he'd just returned from exile to South Africa under an indemnity from prosecution. For Mac's safety, I still could not reveal any more than this. So the pretence had to continue.

'As far as I'm concerned,' I said, 'his arrest is unlawful, since he was under an indemnity granted to all returning ANC leaders. What he's been arrested for, I don't know for certain. All I know is that our family is devastated. We were about to go home this evening.'

At this point, Joey confronted me. Milou was still sucking his thumb. 'Whose arrest, Ma?'

I hadn't realised they had followed me down to the phone. I had considered telling them another story for the moment, to ease their pain, but now the secret was out. What could I say? That their dad had been arrested yesterday, but I was not yet sure why? That as soon as I knew the reasons I would tell them? I thought that would be quite enough of a blow for them to absorb for the time being. So I told them that he would not be in custody for long, as it was an illegal arrest and Uncle Oliver and Uncle Joe would ensure his release soon. Until then, we could go away somewhere nice for a while, if they wanted to.

Milou's reaction shook me. He said nothing, just sucked his thumb harder and stormed off towards his bedroom. Joey began sobbing uncontrollably, which was just as disconcerting. I held her tight as she sobbed in despair, calling out for Mac. I was wracked with their pain, but dared not shed a tear.

I went to check on Milou, who had crawled back into bed. His face was tear-stained, and he still wouldn't talk. Then the phone began to ring incessantly. Journalists, friends, comrades, relatives from South Africa. I was tempted to unplug the phone so I could talk to the children and mull things over, but Milou and Joey wouldn't let me, just in case someone was phoning to say that it was all right for us to come home.

During breakfast, Milou remained silent. Even Joey could not get him to talk. I suddenly remembered we had nowhere to go. Just as I was about to dial our neighbour Nicola to check if her attic was still vacant, a call came through from my landlady, who had just heard of Mac's arrest on the BBC. She said that if we needed to stay on in the house for a while longer, she would be happy to accommodate the new tenant temporarily in one of her other houses. One less complication to handle, I thought, and jumped at the offer.

I suggested to the children that we go to the beach for the day, but first we had to retrieve the odd bits of furniture stored in Nicola's garage to make our place habitable again. We could be here for a very long while yet.

Still in shock, we started to unpack our suitcases.

*　　*　　*　　*　　*

I answered the phone for the umpteenth time that morning. This time it was Ketso, a political activist from South Africa.

'I had no idea Mac was inside South Africa,' he said. 'When Pravin and the others were arrested two weeks ago for Vula activities, you said nothing. Are you okay?'

'I don't know what he's been up to,' I replied, 'but I'm sure his arrest was a mistake.'

It hurt me to have to lie to Ketso, because he was one of the people I would have felt comfortable confiding in, especially as he had been showing such interest in the Vula arrests since they began a couple of weeks ago. It was as if he too were somehow involved.

Ketso had come to Sussex University in 1988 to further his studies, and just two weeks earlier had arranged for a group of South African postgraduate students attending the university's Institute of Development Studies, as well as a few Nicaraguan friends, to have lunch at a pub on the banks of a beautiful stream on the outskirts of Brighton. At the time the fact that Gebuza, Mac's deputy, had been arrested in a safe house had already made the headlines. In the house the police had found communications that referred to an arms build-up, which they assumed was aimed at a military takeover of the country.

At the pub lunch, the children played in the stream under a hot July sun, while we lounged on the grassy banks, glued to the radio for more news. Suddenly it was announced that more Vula activists had just been arrested, including Ketso's uncle, Pravin Gordhan (who was to become Commissioner of the South African Revenue Service). Disturbed by the news, Ketso and the others started asking what this would mean for the safety of other comrades, and for the negotiations. A long discussion ensued. I remained silent, true to my image of a detached, apolitical mom more concerned with the responsibilities of raising her children. I desperately wanted to tell them that Mac was Gebuza's commander and that I was certain, and deeply concerned, that he would be picked up next. But I said nothing.

To avoid any possible problems with the South African police, I was determined to return home 'clean'. They had to think that I was ignorant of Mac's underground work, and had no identity other than as his wife and the mother of his children. Wives in the struggle, even those known to be actively involved, were generally not credited with an identity of their own by the majority of their fellow comrades. Still, it suited me to play the political ignoramus, an 'academic' who'd served international organisations in prestigious jobs, but who was 'ideologically' naive, with no record of 'real' service in the struggle.

* * * * *

I was still quietly unpacking our suitcases with the help of the children when there was a loud knock on the front door. It was 11 a.m. Within seconds there was an even louder knock, and then a frantic call to open the door. I rushed to open it, and standing there were Nanda and his daughter Maya, our friends from Bournemouth, anxious to know how we were taking the news of Mac's arrest. They had driven all the way from Dorset to check on us after catching the story on breakfast TV. They had tried to phone, but the line was constantly engaged. Nanda felt it was important that we not return to South Africa immediately. They had come to take us to their home for a couple of weeks.

The children were overjoyed. They loved Maya's company. At sixteen she was much older than them, but knew exactly how to keep them happy and entertained. If she wasn't telling them a story or taking them for a walk, she'd be involved with them in some art project or other. And Nanda, a lifelong friend of Mac's, always made us feel safe. He and his wife Beverley often invited us to spend weekends with them, taking us under their wing, arranging walks, outings and dinner parties that brought a ray of light to those dark days.

Just as we put Milou's entire collection of *Asterix* comic-books and the skateboard and rollerblades into the car boot and were about to set off for Bournemouth, I remembered my personal telephone directory and all the people I would have to call. I rushed back into the house to find it. The phone started to ring again, but I ignored it.

I was so exhausted I don't remember too much of that drive, except that Milou continued to remain silent for its duration. He was clearly shattered, but, unlike his younger sister Joey, he rarely expressed his feelings, preferring to communicate with me on impersonal matters, like what he'd read in his favourite nature magazines, or what parts he needed to fix my computer, the Hoover or the electric kettle. Even before last night's news, he seemed to be constantly haunted by something he would not share, something that seemed to go beyond his recent bad experiences at his school in Brighton.

'Zee, we're here!' Maya tugged at my sleeve to wake me up as we pulled up outside their house. Without a moment's hesitation the kids put on their rollerblades while Maya went to get hers, and within minutes they were off, down the sloping tree-lined avenues they so enjoyed blading through in this sleepy suburb of Bournemouth. Watching them speed around the bend, I was aghast as Milou, his long hair flying freely in the wind and his antics becoming more daring, narrowly missed bumping into an elderly couple heading in our direction.

In fright the old man dropped his walking stick, but was unable to bend down to pick it up. His wife couldn't do so either, so I rushed to help them. In response, they said angrily that such 'wild darkies' had no place in 'their' town. So this conservative seaside town was indeed only for the 'newlyweds and nearly deads', and racist ones at that, I thought! How sorry I felt for Nanda and Beverley that they had had to leave London and move to this demure dump to keep his job. And now he'd been retrenched anyway. Compared with this conservative place, Brighton was like a breath of fresh air, a vibrant city with a cosmopolitan feel, and just a short drive away from the English Channel, from where one could cross to nearby France and the rest of Europe.

Nanda showed me where we would sleep. He'd put us all together in one large corner room. He knew how much the children and I would need each other to get through this patch. It was already quite late in the afternoon. While we waited for Beverley to return from her publishers, I helped Nanda prepare supper. He was the first man I knew who had happily swapped roles with his wife, doing the housework while she earned an income, teaching and writing children's books. I too was my family's sole breadwinner, but only because, as a full-time freedom fighter, Mac did not earn a cent. In 1980, when I arrived in Lusaka and volunteered for permanent ANC deployment, the then treasurer general of the ANC, Thomas Nkobi, told me that I should support my family in order to relieve the movement from having to do so. I accepted that this was the way things had to be.

'Let's hope I don't need permission from up high to be deployed in a full-time campaign for Mac's release from prison,' I told Nanda as we set the table for supper. 'There's no way I'm going to sit around doing nothing.'

We finished supper early, as the children were tired and I wanted to spend some time with them before they fell asleep. While tucking them in, I urged Milou to take heart from the fact that it was just a question of time before the ANC got Mac out of prison.

'It's not about *when* we see Dad again, but *if* we do,' he retorted angrily, uncharacteristically venting his feelings. 'I'm tired of your lies, lies and more lies! You wouldn't have told us Dad was arrested in

South Africa and not sick in Moscow if Joey hadn't overheard the conversation this morning. I was waiting to see if you would tell us. I heard everything last night.'

I was shocked, yet in a strange way glad that he was letting it all out. His thumb-sucking and tear-stained face last night were the result of overhearing my conversation with Valli.

'All these years you've treated me like the enemy,' he said, his voice rising as tears welled up in his eyes. 'Do you think I didn't know that Dad wasn't in Moscow but underground in South Africa? And I never even told Joey, because you wanted to keep it a secret to protect Dad from being caught, and she wouldn't have been able to keep that secret.'

I was dumbfounded. Over the years he'd quietly picked up that Mac's illness in Moscow was a cover. And, young as he was, he'd played along to make things easier all round. Yet he was deeply saddened to be excluded from something so central to the family's well-being, as if he was an outsider. No wonder he'd stopped communicating with me long ago. He'd found it wiser to remain quiet about his painful sense of exclusion from such important secrets in his own family, instead of confronting me and forcing me to admit the truth. And yet he often told his sister not to give me too much grief, as I already had far too much on my plate. Remarkably, although he'd somehow found out early on that Mac was underground in South Africa and not ill in Moscow, he had never once revealed this to his sister!

'You were too young to be burdened with secrets, Mils,' I pleaded. 'I didn't confide in you because I have to protect you too, not only Dad. And the separation is hurting him as much as it is hurting us.'

Though Mac's goodbye letter was in safekeeping, I told Milou some of what Mac had written to us to try to bolster his courage and lift his mood.

'We're going to win this one, just wait and see. Dad and all of us will be fine, and we'll be home with him before you know it.'

But he refused to be consoled. He didn't want to hear more 'lies'.

'Face the truth, Ma,' he said. 'Dad's more likely to die in jail, the same way they killed Steve Biko. You know how they are.'

Milou knew more than I'd imagined about events in South Africa, simply by overhearing and observing the adults. He must have heard his father talking about how gifted Steve Biko had been, and of the brutal manner of his death. All I could do to try to comfort him was to stroke his head gently while he sucked his thumb and tossed and turned and sobbed, until he fell asleep.

'Not *when* ... but *if* ...' Those words told me all I needed to know about what Milou was going through.

CHAPTER 2

Free Mac Maharaj!

That night I called Vella and Patsy Pillay, old friends and leading members of the international Anti-Apartheid Movement.

'What's the strategy to get Mac out of jail?' I asked them.

'We've tried to reach you in Brighton all day to talk to you about it,' they said. 'Our plan is to start with a demonstration outside South Africa House, demanding Mac's release in two days' time. Then, the day after that, we will demonstrate near Margaret Thatcher's residence at 10 Downing Street.'

I was delighted with this rapid response to Mac's arrest, and felt very impatient to get the ball rolling.

Vella told me that these demonstrations would, between them, be attended by the ANC chief representative in London, Comrade Mendi Msimang, the head of the Labour Party, Neil Kinnock and his wife Glynis, Father Trevor Huddlestone, who'd been associated with our freedom struggle since his days as a priest in Sophiatown, and other ANC and anti-apartheid activists. There would also be radio and TV interviewers, who would ask me to provide some family background and explain the illegality of Mac's arrest. And the children would personally deliver a letter calling for Mac's release to the British Foreign Minister, Mr Douglas Hurd, at his office in Whitehall. I agreed that we would discuss further action to secure Mac's release once I reached London.

The next day Maya organised the materials for the posters we would carry at the demonstration, and she and the children designed and constructed them. 'We want our Dad ... bring him back now!' some of them read. Milou set about writing the letter to Douglas Hurd, asking him to intervene with President de Klerk for his dad's release. The preparation went at a frenetic pace, and by that evening we were packed and ready to set off early the next morning for the first leg of our 'Free Mac Maharaj!' campaign. In South Africa, a similar campaign was afoot at grassroots level.

A huge crowd had gathered outside South Africa House on Trafalgar Square, demanding Mac's immediate release. The mood of defiance, the taunting by the demonstrators of South African High Commission officials peering nervously through the windows – afraid, it seemed, to come out and face us – the chanting of freedom songs and of Mac's name gave me strength. We were not alone. Joey stuck closer than ever to my side, her legs wrapped around my waist like a baby koala bear clinging to its mother. Milou, fortified by the crowd's support, held up his 'We want our dad … Bring him back now!' poster, with his arms reaching as far up into the sky as possible so that everyone could see it. I watched him as he held the poster up, determined to make his point, even when his little arms started aching as much as his heart. Father Huddlestone put his arm around Milou, clearly aware of his pain.

The British and South African media started their questions. 'Mrs Maharaj, why was your husband arrested?' asked the BBC TV interviewer.

'I have just learnt that he was commanding an underground operation in South Africa,' I replied. 'This operation apparently started long before the Groote Schuur talks began last month between the ANC and the South African government for a negotiated settlement. The South African police stumbled on this operation a few weeks ago and have now arrested my husband. His arrest is actually illegal.'

'Why do you say so?'

'First, because an indemnity from prosecution was granted to all ANC leaders for political offences committed before 8 October 1990 so that they would be able to participate in peace negotiations. Vula was implemented in the late eighties. Second, even to this day, there has been no agreement on a date for the cessation of the armed struggle.'

Noting Joey's intense interest in this conversation, I passed her on to Maya to take away, in case the interview became disturbing. I indicated to Milou that he too should move away from my side, but he refused.

'Are you confident that, as part of the negotiations, the ANC will get him out?' the interviewer asked.

'Absolutely,' I said. 'Joe Slovo is key to the ANC negotiations. And I now hear he was one of Mac's commanders in Operation Vula. He will make sure Mac and all the other Vula operatives are freed unconditionally.'

My confidence was unmistakable.

'But an ANC official has just gone on record in another interview we had a few minutes ago saying the ANC had nothing to do with Vula,' the interviewer continued. 'It was a maverick operation neither sanctioned nor supported by the movement.'

I was shocked. Was the ANC washing its hands of Mac because Vula's discovery might scupper the negotiations? But how would this be possible in terms of the indemnity? Either the interviewer briefing me had heard wrong, or there was more to this!

I calmly responded to the statement, even though my heart was racing. 'The operation was presumably so secret that many in the top echelons of the ANC were unaware of it. I myself only got to know about it through Mac's arrest. So it's not surprising that many would say it was not an ANC operation.'

How I wished I could show them Mac's letter to prove that this was not a maverick operation, that OR and JS were deeply involved in Vula and that Mac, though rising to the challenge of the task, had been very nervous about being caught.

'[G]etting into a tight ball of knots is a positive thing,' Mac had written in his goodbye letter, 'because I see it as part of the signs that we are internalising the challenge we face, have accepted the challenge and slowly began [*sic*] to work ourselves into a condition of raring to go at the task.

'Tomorrow it is getting together all the bits and bobs, checking every detail … JS plans to spend the evening with me, then early on Saturday I move. I hope by then to be ready to say: "Boldness, be my friend!" … Remember to give OR your phone no. so that he can keep in touch.'

But I wondered whether the ANC leadership would disown Operation Vula, thus endangering Mac's release from prison.

'Don't think so negatively,' I scolded myself. 'Even with OR so sick, JS will confirm that Operation Vula was OR's baby and that they were its overall commanders when Mac was chosen to see it through.'

An official from the High Commission of South Africa finally emerged to collect our letter addressed to President de Klerk, demanding Mac's release on the basis of the illegality of his arrest. That's when Milou, Joey and I crossed the road from the High Commission to Trafalgar Square, past Nelson's Column and across the square to the Foreign Minister's offices in Whitehall. Milou asked us to stop for a moment as we passed the Changing of the Guard. He wanted a glimpse of the pomp and pageantry and a moment to summon the courage to deliver his letter to Douglas Hurd, who was to receive it in person.

One of Hurd's aides met us outside. Once security had cleared the three of us, we were asked to wait in a reception area. Within minutes the minister appeared. We exchanged greetings and shook hands. Then Milou gave him the letter, and nervously asked him if he would please help get his dad out of prison. Hurd said that he would do his best, and encouraged us to be strong. We returned to our friends waiting for us outside South Africa House. Also present was the official who had told the BBC that Vula was a maverick operation unknown to the ANC.

He confronted me as we approached the group. 'You told the media Vula was an ANC operation when it was not.'

Another comrade at his side chipped in. 'You are *just* the wife of Mac Maharaj. You are not Mac Maharaj. You have no right to talk the way you did!' he said angrily.

Goodness, talk about sexism! It was bad enough to be regarded as 'Mac's wife' and not an individual in my own right with a contribution to make to the struggle – I could handle that. But it was quite another to be made to feel that the support of a wife was irrelevant. This really angered me, as so many political activists drew on the strength and support of their spouses to carry on their work. It was as if holding the family together and other forms of encouragement counted for nothing. As if you were somehow a lesser person if your contribution was not visible! What Mac had said in his letter struck me forcefully: 'It seems you have to be the rock giving strength to Milou, Joey and me ... Your presence by my side and the knowledge that our family, as a family, a single unit is going into battle and not me as an individual, gives me great courage ...'

Sensing the children's panic at this over-the-top and insensitive attack, I replied quietly, 'Your attitude is unfortunate. But you are hardly in the right frame of mind to discuss it now. We will talk another day.'

Maya and Beverley had gathered together our posters and some ANC flags. We went by underground tube with Vella, Patsy, Mike Terry, the secretary of the Anti-Apartheid Movement, and a few other comrades to Patsy's home in East Finchley. Once there, Mike and I discussed the movement's plan for a European campaign agitating for Mac's release. Would I be prepared to give evidence at a specially convened UN Commission on Human Rights meeting? My evidence would become the basis for the UN's intervention with De Klerk. They also needed to know whether I would give more interviews in London and attend demonstrations to keep the pressure on the

British Foreign Office. And what did I think about going to Holland, Germany and Belgium to raise awareness of Mac's plight, speaking at public rallies and to the media, parliamentarians and other government officials? I would have to try to persuade these officials to write to President de Klerk to release Mac.

My consistent answer was that I would do whatever it took for Mac's release. Our family wanted to return to South Africa and to some semblance of normality. We spent the rest of the afternoon finalising my scheduled meetings and interviews in London for the next four days and preparing for the European campaign.

After supper we relaxed and talked over coffee. Joey eventually fell asleep, exhausted as she was by the day's events, and Milou went out to play in the back garden. Anand, Patsy and Vella's eldest son, then a Visiting Professor of Mathematical Logic at the University of Notre Dame in Paris, pitched up with some of his colleagues. Talking with them about their work – I had worked in the same field once – was a wonderfully relaxing diversion for me, but made me forget that Milou was not around. When at 9.30 p.m. he hadn't come in, Patsy went out to call him. She came rushing back in, alarmed. Milou was cutting the ANC flag to shreds and stamping on the pieces. He was unfazed when I stopped him and demanded an explanation.

'First they take my dad away, now they say he wasn't working for them and that you have no right to defend him. Stuff this flag!'

He defiantly stamped on the tatters again. Milou knew a different story from the one he had overheard the official tell that afternoon. It was as if he felt we had been betrayed.

*   *   *   *   *

The next morning, 30 July 1990, BBC radio news announced that Mac, in leg irons and handcuffed to two policemen, had attended his sister's funeral the previous day. This must have been at about the same time we were outside South Africa House. His lawyer, Ismail Ayob, had applied for him to attend the cremation. His sister had died on 28 July, the day after we were to have arrived in South Africa. She was still alive on 25 July, the day Mac was arrested. He had visited her a week earlier, a day or so before he spoke at the official launch of the South African Communist Party, which, like the ANC, had just recently been unbanned.

That afternoon, Ismail Ayob phoned me. He had been trying to get hold of us in Brighton for days. He told us not to come back to South Africa for the moment. He'd just seen pictures of us in South African newspapers at the demonstration outside South Africa House, published alongside the interviews we'd given. He said Mac was being treated as if he was South Africa's Public Enemy No. 1, chained, roughed up and completely denied his dignity, even as the Groote Schuur negotiations for a peaceful settlement were continuing.

Ismail reiterated that it was too risky for me to come home. He agreed to send me pictures of Mac taken at the funeral, but made me promise to keep them from the children, as it would be too harrowing for them to see their dad in chains.

A few days later, I was interviewed on radio for *World News* at the BBC studios near The Strand.

'Your husband's political colleagues must regard him as a hot potato at this point in time,' prodded the interviewer. 'Otherwise by now they would have intervened with President de Klerk, if not for his unconditional release, then at least for him to be charged and granted bail while he awaits trial. Even his Communist Party comrade Joe Slovo has responded with a "no comment". The liberation alliance is surely very embarrassed and uncomfortable?'

This question disturbed me. I wasn't sure what was going on within the leadership in South Africa. But I refused to be drawn in.

'If anyone should be feeling uncomfortable, it's De Klerk and his National Party,' I snapped impatiently, while wondering what was going on at home. 'They are the ones who have contravened the indemnity protecting Mac from arrest, they are the ones who stand to be condemned!'

Once this stage of the petitions, presentations, meetings and interviews was over, we set off for Bournemouth. All the way back I was haunted by that interviewer's question. If Mac was now a hot potato, an embarrassment to the ANC at this delicate point in South Africa's political history, what did that mean for his release? I decided to phone Nelson Mandela at his home once we reached Bournemouth.

Earlier that year, some months following his release from Robben Island and a month or so before Mac's arrest, Madiba had brought to the UK a computer disc with an encoded message from Mac to give to me. At that point Mac was still supposed to be dying in Moscow, so Madiba did not want anyone to know about the disc, or whom it was from. He merely sent word to me that I should try to reach him. This proved impossible, even though we were within a stone's throw of each other twice during his trip to the UK: at the meeting welcoming him and his wife Winnie to London for the first time since his release from prison; and also at the huge concert celebrating his release, at which Tracey Chapman was the main performer.

On both these occasions, the excitement and chaos, the clamour for his attention and the tight security around Madiba prevented me from getting close to him. Even though there were some leading members of the London-based ANC who had access to Madiba that day and who could have helped me reach him, they clearly didn't believe that I had a good enough reason to see him. As far as they were concerned, Mac, whom they knew had grown very close to Madiba in prison, was off the political scene, dying in Moscow of a kidney disease. Of course I could not tell them just why I had to reach Madiba, and once again felt trapped by this need for silence. So, with the children by my side, I took a chance and reversed the truth, telling them that I had an urgent message for Madiba from Mac in Moscow.

One of them in particular did not accept my story, and most

certainly would not have believed me had I decided to tell him that it was, in fact, Madiba who had asked to meet me! In the thrall of Madiba's magic, this bully, who had been close to the thugs who had beaten up my father years ago at Johannesburg's Zoo Lake, had somehow assumed ownership of the world's most revered ex-prisoner, as if he were his gatekeeper, and nobody would get past him.

In frustration I tried to push my way through, but he was unmoveable. I later heard that he had, on several occasions, blocked other comrades who also had good reasons for seeing Madiba. In the end, Madiba, who had no idea how difficult it was for me to reach him, gave up waiting and asked Ahmed Kathrada, his co-prisoner on Robben Island and at Pollsmoor, to do whatever he could to get the encoded disc to me. Fortunately, Kathy made this happen.

We reached Bournemouth at six o'clock on the evening of 30 July 1990. Once I had bathed the children, fed them and put them to bed, I called Madiba's house. A security person answered, and, when I asked to speak to Madiba, asked me to identify myself. Winnie then came on the phone, politely inquired how we were keeping and offered words of encouragement, which I really appreciated. Then she handed the phone to her husband. This would become a pattern whenever I called Madiba.

In his inimitable staccato drawl, he greeted me warmly and asked how we were doing. To my surprise, he even remembered Milou and Joey's names. Of course he knew I was phoning about Mac, because he immediately told me not to worry, that Mac would be fine. He said he'd be visiting Mac the following week, on 7 August, and that plans would be made to get him released. As deputy president of the ANC, Madiba could intervene in this matter. I knew he would do his best. I already felt better.

'But Uncle Nelson,' I said, 'I need to know one more thing. Mac knew it was very likely he would be arrested next after the other Vula arrests. What made him hang around? Couldn't he see the danger?

Could you not have persuaded him to get out for a while, if only for the sake of our children?'

When indemnity from prosecution had been granted to ANC leaders following Nelson Mandela's release from prison in January 1990, he had told Mac to exit the country illegally as soon as possible, and then immediately return legitimately, as if he had never been underground in South Africa. Mac did so in June 1990.

There was a brief pause. 'Your husband is a very courageous man,' Madiba said. 'He knew the danger to himself, but felt he couldn't desert the rest of the team. As the leader of Vula, his arrest would minimise the chances of the others being caught.'

What Madiba didn't tell me on the phone that day is that he and Mac had anticipated his arrest, and that they had jointly decided it best that Mac should face it, especially as Madiba was confident that he would soon be able to get him released.

* * * * *

'I saw Mac last week,' Madiba phoned to tell me on 14 August, Joey's sixth birthday. 'He's okay, a bit roughed up, but in a real fighting mood and unruffled by their interrogation. And as provocative as ever, certainly not prepared to tell them anything.'

'When will he be out, Uncle Nelson?' was all I could ask. 'What have you agreed with the regime?'

'We are insisting that he be released immediately,' Madiba said. 'The red tape around this arrest is enormous. De Klerk is talking to the security apparatus.'

'He was under an indemnity protecting him from arrest and they arrested him,' I complained. 'Under the proposed Pretoria Agreement, political trials are to end. Doesn't this mean that they will have no choice but to release him unconditionally, unless they intend to renege on this agreement too?'

'If the regime is serious about its international image and wants a negotiated end to apartheid, they will have to release him,' Madiba replied. 'We just have to keep up the pressure. They know that they can't ride roughshod over us any more.'

'But have they mentioned a release date?' I urged.

'De Klerk has now promised this will happen by September,' Madiba reassured me. 'For now, let's take that on trust. Please be patient. We'll get Mac out.'

September came and went, and still Mac and his Vula co-accused were being held without access to lawyers, doctors, family or friends under the Internal Security Act, which had effectively been a licence to torture, maim and kill political opponents in secret. I called Madiba more frequently now. Winnie kept answering the phone, supportive as ever, comforting me and then handing over to Madiba.

'We have been hoodwinked about the date of his release,' he explained. 'They have been avoiding me, and I have been unable to get any explanation.'

It was clear that the regime had an agenda. It began to look likely that the detainees were indeed being held as hostages to the talks. I began to wonder what Joe Slovo, one of Mac's Vula commanders, was thinking and doing about his situation. OR was still very ill at the time.

Madiba must have told Walter Sisulu about my concern, because Oom Walter phoned me out of the blue one day.

'We understand your concern, my dear,' he said. 'We are doing all we can to get Mac out, but the regime is playing games. They had promised by September. But we know what we're up against. We will not give up.'

I desperately needed his reassurance. I knew that political giants such as Mandela and Sisulu would not give up on their comrade just because his untimely arrest might put the ANC at a disadvantage in the negotiations. The thought of what countless struggle wives had been through also helped me get a perspective on the matter.

*   *   *   *   *

'You're so gaunt! God, you've lost so much weight!' exclaimed Connie Braam of the Dutch Anti-Apartheid Movement as I entered the arrivals lounge at Schiphol Airport in Amsterdam. It was October 1990, and I was in Holland to start the 'Free Mac Maharaj' campaign, orchestrated by the powerful network of European Anti-Apartheid Movement activists.

Connie and I knew each other from the early seventies, when I was a performer in the ANC's London-based cultural group, Mayibuye. The group gave shows across Europe, especially following the Soweto Uprising of 1976, an event around which we raised awareness in Europe about the struggle in South Africa in song and poetry. Our performances had captured the hearts and minds of the growing European audiences, who kept asking for us to be invited back.

Connie took me to a tiny hotel in central Amsterdam, which would be my base. She explained the hectic schedule that had been arranged. President de Klerk would also be interviewed on Dutch TV once he arrived in Holland later that week. I saw my television interview as a great opportunity to expose his government's double standards and dishonesty.

At my first meeting with the Development Committee of the Dutch parliament in The Hague, I explained that Mac and Billy Nair, the veteran trade unionist from Natal, were two of at least 103 persons detained indefinitely without trial under the Internal Security Act, which had served as a cover for the murder and torture of political prisoners.

'Get them out of there!' I pleaded. 'Let them be charged if necessary, even if it's for treason, and intervene for their bail.'

I felt that they would be safer in the public spotlight rather than holed up in police cells without access to anyone.

'Detention without trial is a travesty of justice compounding the illegality of their arrests!' I stated vehemently, to underscore the unfairness of the situation.

How could De Klerk be seeking a negotiated end to apartheid when there was still an armoury of repressive laws in force, when police shootings in Sebokeng and other townships were still happening, when thousands of political prisoners still languished in jail? These obstacles to free political activity, like the Vula arrests, had to be removed if De Klerk's offer of peaceful negotiations was to be taken in good faith, and if the suspicion that he was using the detainees and prisoners as hostages to the talks was to be lifted.

I said that surely De Klerk could not believe that South Africa had moved from international pariah to messiah just because economic sanctions had forced him and his cabinet to release Nelson Mandela, Walter Sisulu, Ahmed Kathrada and other prominent political prisoners. He had to go further and put his money where his mouth was by creating the conditions for free political activity.

This patent display of bad faith by the apartheid regime was the refrain of the 'Free Mac' campaign. It was the mantra I repeated to the European media, politicians and general public alike – backed intermittently with more personal and political detail, depending on what else they wanted to know.

A groundswell of support for the release of the Vula detainees was becoming obvious from that very first meeting with the Dutch parliamentarians, who wasted no time in contacting De Klerk to release them. With that kind of support and the support of the likes of Joe Slovo and Nelson Mandela, Mac and his co-detainees would be released in no time, I thought happily. I could hardly wait to hear when our life in limbo would end and we could start making some plans. My life had been on hold and I a lady-in-waiting since the beginning of the eighties, and it was beginning to wear me down.

In his interview on Dutch TV, De Klerk insisted that it was a condition of a peaceful settlement that the ANC should lay down its arms. That was the reason why the Vula operatives had been arrested. In my interview, I stated that De Klerk's armies hadn't laid down their weapons, and in any case, a date for a ceasefire hadn't yet been agreed on. The majority of the Dutch people did not doubt the justice of the national liberation cause, and the Madiba magic was already entrancing the world. My views therefore garnered more sympathy than De Klerk's. This became very clear in subsequent media reports and the messages of support I received.

My pleas in Bonn and other German cities were also taken seriously; I called on the German government to intervene with De Klerk for Mac's release, and it fell on unexpectedly sympathetic ears. A very influential foreign ministry official faxed De Klerk, demanding Mac's immediate release, failing which South Africa would face trade sanctions from Germany. Ingeborg Vick, the head of Germany's Anti-Apartheid Movement, kept telling me how amazingly well we'd done to achieve that. Apparently this man was an arch-conservative who had previously been staunchly opposed to the Anti-Apartheid Movement!

Support was growing so well in Germany that Ingeborg asked me to extend my stay to maximise this opportunity. But my children had been left with relative strangers in Brighton for too long. A few days more would stretch their and my heartstrings to breaking point. I couldn't. I needed to be with them, as I knew they needed to be with me. Since the Belgian leg of the trip had not materialised, and I had achieved my mission to get the Dutch and Germans to intervene with De Klerk, I felt justified at this point in refusing their request to stay on in Germany. Instead, I went home.

CHAPTER 3

Graçias á la Vida

The children, still devastated, were back at school. It was now October, and the cold English winter we had hoped to avoid had set in. It was winter in more ways than one. Joey was admitted to the Brighton Paediatric Hospital with 'juvenile arthritis' in her ankles and knees, but after intensive tests, no physical cause could be found for her condition. The paediatrician concluded that it must be 'stress-induced', caused psychosomatically.

'Does this child have any reason to be upset?' he asked me. I told him how much Joey missed her father and how he'd been jailed on the eve of our reunion with him.

'That explains it,' the doctor said. 'There's not much more we can do for her here, unfortunately.'

But fortunately for Joey, and unlike her brother, when anguish hit her, she wore her heart on her sleeve. She did not try to rationalise or hide her emotions. She wanted to talk about the problems and get them off her chest.

Around that time, Milou, in a reverie on a first-floor window ledge, lost his balance and fell. He was hurt badly enough to be kept in bed, but not hospitalised. He had already missed six months of school at the beginning of the year, when the Sussex County Council had reneged on their promise to accept both the children at Balfour Road School, and had admitted only Joey. Those six months out of school, in a strange place with too much time to worry about his father, marked the beginning of a deep withdrawal into himself that was to go on for many years to come. At the same time I was preoccupied not only with the 'Free Mac' campaign, but also fighting a court case to get the school to admit Milou; and his sister was making friends and, on the face of it, settling into her new environment.

Later we learnt that one of the major causes of Milou's deep emotional trauma was his belief that Mac's work in South Africa was so worthy and important that he had no right to feel upset or angry about not having a father around. He thought it was selfish of him not to want to share Mac with others. This made him repress and deny his pain. It was becoming increasingly clear to me that no matter how good I tried to be as a mother, I could never be a father to Milou.

While Milou was recovering from his fall, Mac's younger brother Kithar phoned from South Africa.

'Zarina, Mac's in hospital with a damaged neck from being tortured,' he told me. 'He's chained by his ankles to his hospital bed at St Aidan's [in Durban], handcuffed and under police guard. But we are able to steal in to visit him and take him food and other things, depending on which nurses are on duty and who is guarding him. Some of the nurses and policemen support us all the way. Madiba has also visited him in hospital.'

'How badly is he hurt?' I asked tensely.

'The doctors are still checking that out. But his neck is in traction,' Kithar said.

I was livid. This meant the torture had exacerbated the injury to the vertebra Mac had suffered in detention. There was nothing I could do from England, except ask Kithar to tell Mac that the children would be writing to him, that we loved him and knew it was now just a matter of time before he was free. It made no sense to me that they kept him chained up, even under police guard. I could only surmise that they saw him as a valuable hostage to the talks, around whose imprisonment they could perhaps gain concessions, and they were afraid he might escape.

'He'll actually be phoning you,' Kithar said. 'Some of those black policemen and nurses risk their jobs when they let him use the phone. They'll get into serious trouble if they're ever found out.'

I asked Kithar whether Elsabe Wessels had managed to deliver the blue tracksuit I'd sent to Mac three months ago. Elsabe had told me she could get the tracksuit to Mac if I arranged to get it to her.

'Yes,' Kithar said, 'I've seen him wear it, and he looks just great in it.'

This made me feel much better, as that tracksuit was a special parting gift from me to Mac when he went underground. But because it was so unique and noticeable, Gebuza had advised him against wearing it, as it would attract too much attention. Mac took the advice and left the tracksuit with me in Lusaka. When I learnt of his arrest from Valli Moosa, I decided to have embroidered on the back of its top the words: 'Graçias á la Vida!' (loosely translated, 'Here's to life!'), and to get the tracksuit to him through Elsabe, Valli's wife-to-be.

'Graçias á la Vida' was our song, written by the Chilean songstress Violeta Parra, and made famous by her daughter Isabella Parra and Victor Jara, a brilliant musician who used his voice and guitar to mobilise the Chilean people against the dictator Augusto Pinochet, who had just toppled the democrat Salvador Allende from power. Pinochet had Victor Jara brutally killed for rallying the Chileans against his dictatorship with his political lyrics and songs. I knew Mac would read into those embroidered words my message to him, that I was there for him and keeping very strong.

'When will Mac be phoning me, Kithar?' I couldn't wait to hear first hand from Mac what was happening to him, to the negotiations and to our future together. But Kithar couldn't say.

I wondered whether I should I tell the children the good news, and whether I should let them talk to him too. It might endanger the nurses and policemen who were already at risk for letting him use the phone.

I asked Kithar's advice. 'Should I let Mils and Joey in on this?'

'Not as yet,' was his answer.

I had to think about this. Living on hold and on the edge had got to us. A kind of battle weariness had been setting in. Even before Mac had gone underground in South Africa, his movements throughout the eighties had been so unpredictable that, each time he returned home, our family had to adjust anew to having him back. Just as soon as we got used to being with him, he would have to leave again. It was like having to dance to a different rhythm each time. As an ANC family we were aware that we were not alone in this situation, but we still found it difficult to have to change step each time.

And now in Brighton, when we needed them most, we saw less of the people who had been there 'for us' when Mac was around. It was as if only those in our family who were celebrated in news headlines really deserved their time. I slowly began to realise that, like the widows and children of those stalwarts who had been hailed as heroes for their selfless contribution to the struggle when they were alive, we could just as easily be forgotten if anything happened to Mac.

The wives of political activists seemed to be perceived as expendable appendages of their husbands, and were generally presumed buried with them when they died. I preferred to think that women were just assumed to be able to cope with anything, and were left to get on with it.

I decided I would let the children talk to Mac when he phoned. I would not tell them where he was calling from and under what conditions. It was as much their right as mine to hear his voice again. They could tell him how they felt, and hear from him how he was doing. And that's exactly what happened. Over the course of the next few weeks, Milou and Joey, sworn to secrecy, spoke to him a couple of times.

But we still had no idea what Mac's fate would be. Even his brother Kithar and sister-in-law Mayna, who were seeing him in secret and smuggling food to him, had no idea. But their brave and unconditional support for Mac, and their warm and informative phone calls, kept us going during that dark spell.

Around this time, I contacted Channel 4's popular prime-time four-minute slot *Speak Your Mind*, which flighted just before the evening news at 7.30 p.m. I wanted this opportunity to remind the British public about Mac's plight. The producer at the time, Andrew Solomon, gave me the slot after he'd heard my speech. After recording the show in London one afternoon, I went to visit OR, who was now out of hospital and at his North London home, under the care of his wife Adelaide.

Mrs Tambo welcomed me when I got there, but asked me not to stay too long, as OR was still too ill to cope with long visits. Ill as he was, though, his warmth thawed the chill of that afternoon. The hugs he gave me that day were the last I would ever receive from him. They made up for the difficulty he had speaking, due to the stroke.

OR asked after the children and was aware of Mac's situation. Painstakingly he assured me that Madiba would not rest until Mac was free. When Mrs Tambo came to tell me that I had exceeded my time, OR wouldn't let me go. We continued talking for another fifteen minutes. It was as if he knew we would never meet again.

He repeated what he had told us the night before Mac left Zambia with Gebuza to enter South Africa: that theirs was a profound act of bravery and dedication. I knew then that OR was not about to disown Vula and Mac because the peace talks might be jeopardised. If OR had been well enough, he would certainly have been among the ANC leaders trying so hard to secure Mac's release. As it transpired, there were some who did not want Mac to walk free.

During my visit, I couldn't help but recall another of OR's kind and caring gestures. In 1989, when I'd developed a 'post-traumatic' cataract of the eye, which half-blinded me, after a car accident I was involved in, OR wasted no time getting me to a top eye surgeon in Moscow to try to save my eyesight. He even sent an overcoat to the airport so that I wouldn't feel the cold on arrival in the Soviet Union! This show of compassion had made a huge difference to my morale and that of the children, and to my resolve to keep going.

*   *   *   *   *

On Thursday 8 November 1990, Mac, Gebuza and their co-accused were charged with terrorism and released on bail. This was as a direct result of Madiba's interventions and the unrelenting international pressure from politicians and public alike, as well as from the ANC and its alliance partners, COSATU and the South African Communist Party. The trial was set for 15 January 1991, in spite of the Pretoria Agreement.

The continuation of this case made a mockery of all the agreements that had been put in place to get the peace process on track. The stringent bail conditions confined Mac and his co-accused to fixed addresses, and they had to report daily to specific police stations, making them vulnerable to attack from the unidentified death squads at work at the time.

More work was now needed to try to stop the illegal trial. I contacted the people in Britain and Europe who had helped secure Mac's bail, asking them to intensify the pressure on the South African government to drop the case. Meanwhile, with Mac out on bail, it became possible for us to consider a visit to South Africa. Not knowing whether the trial would be dropped and, if it took place, what the outcome would be, a permanent return home was no longer on the agenda at this stage. I would need advice on whether even a visit would be a good idea.

'Hey, Boks, I'm out.' Mac was on the phone that same Thursday evening of his release. 'You and the kids can come home.'

I put the children on the line. To our surprise, Joey stated firmly that a visit was all she was interested in.

'You cannot move me again just like that,' she told her dad. 'I've got used to living here. I will chain myself to the tree outside and you'll have to come and cut the tree down to get me to leave Brighton.'

Unlike Milou, she would later tell Mac quite openly that no matter what beautiful things he said to convince her otherwise, he had actually chosen the struggle over her. She was still too young then to see it any other way. And the shock of having been stopped in our tracks just as we were about to return home had made her wary of any such plans.

But Milou was desperate to leave Brighton in order to be with his dad as soon as possible. Joey's sentiments made me think of the poet Lord Byron's words: 'My very chains and I grew friends, / So much a long communion tends, / To make us what we are:- even I, / Regain'd my freedom with a sigh.' As it happened, we would not be gaining our freedom for a while yet. For a start, Mac's stringent bail conditions restricted him to the magisterial district of Johannesburg.

The children and I decided that this time I would not pull them out of school to go home, because we might have to return to Brighton after the 1990/91 Christmas holidays. We would leave for South Africa when school broke up on 19 December, six weeks hence. I would use the time to try to get Mac's case dropped, to get an extension on the rental of the house and to fully recover my health. Living in exile in such uncertainty had exhausted me. I called it combat fatigue.

Yet the news of Mac's release on bail had already stirred a renewed optimism and energy in all of us. We were becoming really excited, but tried to temper it with caution. In the ten years of our marriage up to then, we were lucky to have spent even half of that time together, counting the days when Mac was not in the front-line states, overseas on missions or undergoing military training, working in the South African underground or in prison. Such lost time together ... some families never made it up, as a partner disappeared, died or sought a divorce. This was a stark feature in the lives of all families in the war against apartheid. We felt lucky to have this chance to try to make up some of that lost time.

Over the next six weeks, Mac found somewhere for us to live, as he had lost the house we were meant to move into in July 1990. He also began to investigate the political machinations behind his long detention in the midst of a peace process. And he began to prepare for his trial in January 1991.

* * * * *

Milou, Joey and I reached Heathrow Airport from Brighton at 6 p.m. on 18 December 1990 for our nine o'clock flight that night. While quietly sipping a cup of coffee, I was approached by photographers from the London *Observer*, a British Sunday newspaper. Their editor had just that morning received a short article I had written about the Vula saga, together with a couple of photos of the family, as well as my covering note saying that I was leaving for South Africa that night with my children. They wanted a more recent photo of us, and had come to take a picture, if we didn't mind. We let them.

One of the photographers made an observation about the size of our suitcases. 'Why are they so small? This is the type of baggage people carry on a short trip away. You're returning home after years in exile, aren't you?'

It would have taken time to explain that we were actually not returning permanently – yet. As we were also so conditioned to the possibility that we might receive a last-minute phone call telling us to unpack our suitcases and stay put, it would be easier to unpack smaller bags. So I just smiled and bid the photographers goodbye. Then we set off for the departure lounge, delighted that we were actually making it home at last, with Mac out of prison, alive and waiting for us.

We marched through the boarding gate like soldiers who'd survived a battle. We'd also march across new bridges in the changing terrain that was South Africa when we came to them. And as the time was nearing for me to start reclaiming my own rhythm, we'd have to cross that bridge too. And who knew, Mac and I might eventually even dance in step again!

It was only once the aeroplane was airborne and we were allowed to unfasten our seatbelts that the realisation fully hit me: we were really going home! For the first time since Valli's chilling phone call I dared feel a glimmer of excitement. The fact that Mac was under a banning order restricting him to the magisterial district of Johannesburg did not dampen the anticipation one bit. What had often looked like a distant dream, of being back in my beloved Jozi and reunited as a family, was almost a reality!

I had often imagined the streets of Fordsburg, where I had spent my childhood. During the seventies, when my attempts to return home were twice refused by the South African visa authorities in London, I wondered whether I would ever walk those streets again. How would they look now? Would my house and school have survived the bulldozers that tore down central Fordsburg and Freedom Square (Red Square's later name) to make place for an Indian commercial centre, the Oriental Plaza? How would this have changed the old Fordsie culture and buzz? How had the struggle changed it? How wonderful that we could now choose to live near non-racial Sacred Heart College. My excitement was mounting. I was not going home a moment too soon!

My thoughts turned to my late mother, as they always do at emotional moments in my life. She would have seen our return home as a triumph of the long haul over the quick fix; of steadfastness over surrender; of hope over despair; of picking up the pieces, as she had always strived to do. I have a vivid, enduring image of her literally picking up the pieces, in this case an antique Chinese porcelain urn that belonged to her wealthy madam. One day, when my mother was a cook/housekeeper in Wigmore Street, London, I observed the madam's son being rude to her. In a rage, I threw an apple at the boy, but it bounced off the wall and shattered the urn. I watched my mother painstakingly restore the urn to its original condition (or so it appeared) with Bostik. It saved her the job. I came to see this incident as a metaphor for my mother's life: fighting to hold things together, even when at times they seemed broken beyond repair.

As we flew home that night, I drew strength from this memory, bracing and mentally preparing myself for the heavy toll that would be exacted from us if Mac were to be found guilty of terrorism. Given how she had steeled herself in the raging fire of her own tumultuous life, my mother Jo would have faced down this threat with the quiet courage and dignity that had become my inspiration. So who was Jo?

PART II

Jo and the Shattered Urn

CHAPTER 4

Boots and all

TROYEVILLE

My mother Josephine was born in 1915 in Cape Town. Her mother was Christine Bain, and her father, Joseph Medell, had apparently been adopted as an infant by a family of fishermen. Jo was raised in Parow, a northern suburb of Cape Town, as an Afrikaans-speaking Christian. Both Christine and Joseph were considered to be 'Cape Coloureds'.

A time came when Jo's parents could no longer afford to raise their seven children, so Jo, the eldest at eight, was given to one of her mother's sisters, who could not have children of her own. Aunt Sarah and her German husband doted on my mother, even feeding her meat – a treat her own parents reserved for adults – and spoiling her with gifts and beautiful clothes. She even went to school.

Then, at the age of eleven, when Jo was in Standard 2, Aunt Sarah died unexpectedly. Her husband left the Cape, and my mother had to return to her parents and help her father raise her younger siblings, while her mother worked as a live-in domestic/cook miles away in Worcester.

When Jo was thirteen, her mother got a job close to home, and Jo was invited to live in a Catholic convent in Paarl run by nuns, most of whom were Italian. The nuns treated her as if she were one of their own, smothering her with love, as Aunt Sarah had done. They claimed to know something of her father Joseph's real parents, and their background. They told Jo that her father was born out of wedlock in the 1890s to one of the daughters of the influential House of Orsini in Milan in northern Italy. Soon after his birth, the infant was shipped out to South Africa under a shroud of secrecy, in the care of a nun. Once there, he was found a foster family. Though this story was never independently verified, it greatly influenced the way the nuns treated Jo while she lived at the convent.

The nuns' unusually progressive views on the First World War, the Anglo-Boer War, and the treatment of South Africa's indigenous peoples by the British and the Boers, emanating from their belief in the 'oneness of all God's children', made a deep and lasting impression on her.

Jo later married out of her religion, race and culture. In 1935, racism had not yet been institutionalised in law, and Jo was engaged to a rich Afrikaner farmer – apparently the only one in the region who owned a much-coveted symbol of wealth and social status: a gramophone. This was at a time when such marriages, though not yet illegal, were taboo.

My father, Amod Abdul Carim, turned up on her convent doorstep out of the blue one fateful day in early 1935, when Jo was just eighteen years old. A handsome young entrepreneur quick to spot an opportunity, he was selling black armbands and ties – made under his instructions by his sisters in Johannesburg, where he lived – to mourn the recent passing of King George V of England. With his gift of the gab, Ami had already sold many of the armbands and ties in other parts of South Africa.

Jo was bowled over by the handsome young Indian. She told me later it had been love at first sight for both of them. But her family was not impressed by this 'Moor' (Muslim infidel), and such a dark-skinned one at that!

So Jo broke off her engagement and she and Ami eloped, going into hiding with a Malay family in District Six. Rachmat and her husband Moegsien were dear friends of Ami's, and they arranged for an Imam to marry Jo and Ami secretly under Muslim rites. My parents remained in hiding from my mother's outraged Christian folks until they could move to Johannesburg, where my father's family, themselves ardent religionists, were waiting expectantly to meet her. Jo was soon accepted into Ami's very strict Muslim family because of her readiness to convert to Islam, her genuine attempts to embrace the culture of her in-laws, which included donning full cover-up garb and learning the art of Indian cuisine, and, not least, because of her alabaster-like complexion, seen by them not only as very beautiful, but also as a mark of social status.

Adjusting to a life so different from the culture and religion in which she had been raised was not easy, keen as Jo was to endear herself to it. For one, the mouth and stomach ulcers she suffered for six months from the hot curries she had never previously eaten were excruciating! But for Jo this was the smallest of sacrifices, so much in love was she with my father – who had broken off his engagement to a very rich Indian woman to marry my mother.

'You don't sit on the fence in life,' she would often tell me as I was growing up. 'You make a commitment one way or the other, and then go for it, boots and all.'

*   *   *   *   *

By the time I was born at 12C Nourse Street in Troyeville, Johannesburg, just as the Second World War was ending, Jo already had four sons, ranging in age from eight years to fifteen months. At the time, she was single-handedly running a small fruit and vegetable shop, which Ami had acquired using her 'white' papers in what, at the time, was a residential area for very poor white people, predominantly Afrikaners and Portuguese.

Ami was in and out of different jobs, failing to stick to any of them. At one point he worked with his father in Diagonal Street, Johannesburg, a privilege that didn't last, as his dad, an astute businessman – the first person to import Persian carpets into South Africa – could not abide the lack of focus his son was displaying. By now Ami had already begun his philandering. He would disappear for months on end, especially when Jo was pregnant, leaving her to look after the children and run the Troyeville fruit and vegetable business on her own. She worked herself to the bone, first to make ends meet and later to turn the shop into a thriving business, while he made irregular financial 'contributions' towards our upkeep from his obsessive gambling.

'The autumn leaves drift by my window, those autumn leaves of red and gold,' crooned Nat King Cole hauntingly from Jo's gramophone in the shop for the umpteenth time one day. Music was the one thing that kept her sane and made her happy when she was sad, and her current idol was Nat. If it wasn't her records, then it was the radio stations that blared out the latest music hits. She knew each word of every song, and often sang along. Right from birth I was immersed in the sounds of the popular music of the day.

One of Jo's Afrikaner customers, Marike, who had heard the records in the shop and fell big-time for Nat King Cole, asked her if she could borrow his most popular hits. Marike took the records home and for the first time realised from his picture on one of the covers that he was black. She was devastated. Could a black man really have a voice like that? She stormed back to the shop, screaming at Jo as she entered, 'You never told me he was a *kaffir*!' Then she threw the records at Jo. As they fell to the ground, Jo went to pick them up, but Marike shoved her out of the way and stamped on them in a frenzy, smashing Jo's hard-earned, much treasured Nat King Cole collection to pieces. Jo threatened to call the police.

Jeffrey, Jo's domestic helper of many years, walked into this fracas carrying me in his arms. With us was a relative of Jeffrey's, whom Jeffrey's young sister had been working for for many years, someone he really wanted to introduce to Jo. The relative, a very distinguished-looking man, had witnessed the entire scene. Marike looked the stranger up and down as she stomped out of the shop, then paused for a moment and turned to Jo.

'Kaffirboetie, you won't see me here any more!'

Jo swallowed her tears.

'I too love Nat King Cole,' said Sam Ngoma, Jeffrey's uncle, while Jo composed herself. 'If it would help, I'll get Jeffrey to bring you some of my collection to listen to until you replace yours,' he offered.

Thus began their exchange of records, with Jeffrey as the intermediary, which was to continue for many years. It was through Sam Ngoma that Jo first got to hear the jazz of Duke Ellington, Billie Holiday, Count Basie, Dizzy Gillespie, Ella Fitzgerald, Charlie Parker, Johnny Hodges and the like.

Marike's abuse was nothing new to Jo. This sort of thing had been going on since she first took over the shop from the previous Portuguese owner, when it was failing as a business. Our windows were smashed and the neighbourhood kids regularly beat up my brothers.

One day, aged two, I was sitting next to the pavement in the gutter, cooling down in the stream of water the heavy rains had brought earlier that day. A speeding truck made a beeline for me, as if to run me over. Instead it hit Jeffrey just as he picked me up and tossed me to safety on the pavement. He was badly hurt, but eventually made a full recovery. The hit-and-run truck driver got away with it, because Jo could not trace him. Everyone in the neighbourhood Jo asked denied witnessing the incident, in spite of all the Nourse Street traffic that day.

Once Jo had saved up enough money, she moved us to a flat in Jajbhay's Building in Market Street, Johannesburg, nearer to the Gold Street Indian Primary School, which my brothers had been attending. My first primary school was the Ferreirastown Indian Primary, which I attended for a year in 1950, before our next move.

CHAPTER 5

Home and away

FORDSBURG

It was a late Saturday afternoon in November 1957 at our home in Fordsburg. The party I had thrown with my school friends to celebrate the end of the school year was in full swing, to the glorious sounds of Elvis Presley's 'Jailhouse Rock'. The next moment my father, supported by two men acting as crutches, limped into the house. His face was bloated to twice its normal size, unrecognisable from the swelling, bruises and cuts.

Blood was pouring from the gashes in his top lip, through which some of his teeth protruded gruesomely. There was a collective shocked gasp. Someone switched off the music. I rushed to help my dad to his bedroom. My younger sister screamed for my mother to come from the kitchen. I asked my friends to leave. Jo came running in, freaking out as she saw this apparition that was her husband Ami.

'I think I know who did this,' she announced angrily to his companions. Then she suddenly became more hushed and pensive. 'I really can't take this any more, I can't go on like this,' her voice trembled.

Realising my sister and I were watching and listening intently, she composed herself and took control of the situation.

'Call the doctor and bring ice, Dettol and cotton wool,' she instructed us while laying Ami down on the bed with the help of the two men who had brought him in. That's when she noticed that his arm and wrist were broken.

'They mean business,' she whispered to him, as she began to clean the blood from his face, ear and neck.

Dr Rajah arrived. A family friend who was also my father's bridge partner – they were awesome together at poker too – he gave my dad a powerful painkilling injection, then drove him to Baragwanath Hospital. As they left, Jo sank into the armchair at the foot of their bed. Not wanting to distress us further, she tried to hold back her tears, but couldn't.

It was not just the shock of seeing Ami in such a state. Jo was always trying to stop us from becoming inured to the violence that we so often encountered living in Fordsburg. Singlehandedly, with little support from my father, she had struggled to raise my four older brothers – now ranging in age from fourteen to nineteen – my younger sister of eleven, and me, in traditions and values from which Ami had long been drifting. She could not abide the physical fights – to settle personal scores or express racial and ethnic resentments – that were commonplace in Fordsburg. This was yet another setback to her efforts to shield us from trouble and keep us focused on work and school.

Neighbours were already gathering around Jo to calm her down. Still shaken, she confided to them that this looked like the start of a new cycle of violence, following an incident that had occurred at a picnic on a scorching Sunday the week before. Barred by law from public swimming pools and with no access to other 'whites only' recreational facilities, we would often end up at a picnic spot used by Coloureds and Indians on the banks of the Jukskei River.

On this particular Sunday morning, Ami accompanied us. He, Jo and the three youngest children – Adam, Shirene and I – set off for Mia's Farm with our swimming costumes and a packed picnic basket. As soon as we arrived there, I changed, impatient to swim in the cool, murky brown river. I insisted on going ahead of the others.

I was an innocent thirteen-year-old girl in a swimming costume walking towards the river on her own, something I had done many times before. As I passed a group of older boys, I was shocked by their taunts and jeers.

'Hey, Bushie!' they shouted at me. 'Good girls don't wear outfits like that in public. But then what do half-castes like you know about what's good anyway?'

I started walking faster but they followed me, continuing their jibes and insults. Eventually my father caught up with me, but still they did not stop. Ami threatened to beat them up, but they just laughed at him. By now I was too upset to swim, so I turned to go back to my mother.

Even with Ami by my side, they continued to follow me, giggling and making lewd comments about my pubescent body. No longer able to hold back the tears, I burst out crying. At this my father grabbed the ringleader and slapped him hard across the face. The others ran to fetch the boy's father, who came threateningly at Ami, hurling more obscenities at us. My dad, equally livid, punched the man in the face. The fight got worse, attracting a big crowd, many egging them on to 'go for it'. The other man finally landed on the ground with a black eye, his mouth and nose bleeding. Ami took my hand and we walked away.

Jo, deeply upset by the name-calling and the fisticuffs, wasted no time in packing up the car with our picnic paraphernalia, rounding up Adam and Shirene, and driving us all out of Mia's Farm at high speed in our 1954 Chevrolet. That had been the week before.

'I'm going to the police today,' she told my dad and Dr Rajah when they returned from Baragwanath.

'It won't be necessary,' Ami replied. 'The matter has already been reported and will be handled my way.'

Two days later, I noticed him cleaning his revolver, a German Luger. I told Jo. She warned Ami that it would only make things worse to go after the thugs who had beaten him up. He assured her that nothing of the kind was going to happen. But all that week he sat on the front stoep with his loaded Luger, as if expecting trouble.

'My nerves can't handle this any more,' Jo told our next-door neighbour, Aunt Hallima, the wife of our landlord, who was like a sister to her. Although her family had by now forgiven Jo for 'shaming' them by breaking up with her influential fiancé and running off with my father, none of them lived nearby.

'Ami's gambling is getting worse. He hardly gives me money for the house, he's never really here for us and now this,' Jo complained, as she slugged four instead of two teaspoons of the neurophosphates Dr Rajah had prescribed a month ago for her collapsing nerves. This had followed another violent incident involving one of my brothers.

I had been walking with Doolie in Market Street, just outside the Johannesburg City Hall, on our way home from Doornfontein. It was about 3 p.m. on a Saturday afternoon. Doolie being very dark-skinned, and I very fair, a group of young, big-built Afrikaners approached us and called out to him, 'Hey, *koelie*, what you freaking doing with a white *cherrie*?'

'I'm his sister!' I screamed hysterically, realising the trouble we were in from earlier incidents like this, but they didn't want to know.

Doolie's own attempts to tell them we were siblings also drew a ferocious 'Liar!' and within moments Doolie was lying on the pavement, being kicked and trampled on by each of them in turn as they continued to hurl more racist abuse. I shouted to passers-by for help, but they just crossed the road to the other side.

'And you shouldn't even be on our streets in the centre of town, *kerriebek*! Stay in your own freaking areas!'

When I pleaded with them to stop assaulting Doolie, they laughed and took it in turns to slap me around. Then one of the boys twisted my arm behind my back and held it there, occasionally twisting it until I would scream in pain.

'Apologise for mixing with blacks and promise you won't do it again,' he mocked me.

Instead I continued to call out for help, hoping some passer-by would have the guts to intervene. Eventually a white man brandishing a *sjambok* appeared. He threatened to skin them alive if they did not leave immediately. The boys ran off, cursing the man. He gave Doolie his handkerchief to staunch the blood from the cut above his eye, and offered us a lift. We asked to be dropped at my aunt's place in Kholvad House, Market Street, as it was fairly close by, and we knew Jo was not at home because it was her day to sell her home-made pies and rotis door to door.

My rich, haughty aunt, Ami's eldest sister, favoured us according to the hue of our skin. She was as welcoming as ever towards me, but clearly not too pleased to see my brother. But because she couldn't drive and Doolie felt too weak to walk home, we waited in her house until early evening, when Jo got home and was able to borrow my father's car to fetch us. She did not even bother to respond when my aunt complained that we always seemed to be getting into trouble, and to be sinking deeper into it the poorer we became. She insinuated that it was Jo who was not raising us properly.

'Things are really coming to a head,' Jo said quietly as she drove us to Dr Rajah's home for the stitches Doolie might need.

* * * * *

After sitting on the stoep with his loaded revolver for the third night running, Ami, still badly hurt, went to rest in bed. No sooner had he dozed off than a group of young men – about four or five of them – arrived at our front door.

They were no more than eighteen or nineteen years old. I recognised some of them from the incident at Mia's Farm. But it was clear they were not here for a fight. One had a broken leg and was on crutches, another was in a neck brace, his head covered in bloodstained bandages. Another boy had a broken arm, one a broken nose and stitches in his forehead, and most of them had swollen faces and black eyes. Talk about a rogue's gallery!

The boys told Jo that Sharif Khan and a certain Mr Mayet,

notorious gangsters of the day with whom Ami was friendly, had instructed them to pay Ami a visit and apologise for assaulting him the previous Saturday. Jo went to wake Ami up and led the boys to the bedroom. Ami was not at all surprised to see the state they were in, as his mobster buddies had apparently assured him that whoever had assaulted him would be given a hiding from hell. Still, Ami did not drop his guard. These, after all, were the 'Becker Street Boys', an Indian gang notorious for its viciousness.

They filed past Ami one by one, each apologising for what they'd done. The spokesperson for the gang, a certain Poenie, explained that they had had no choice but to defend the honour of the man Ami had punched to the ground.

'What about my daughter's honour?' Jo asked them quietly.

They had no answer.

*   *   *   *   *

Adam was expelled from school later that year, following in the footsteps of Doolie, who had just the previous year been expelled for his insolence towards the teachers, and for not turning up for class. All of our teachers were white, but clearly insufficiently qualified to teach at the better-paid white schools. A few of them were hardcore racists who had no qualms about calling us names, such as *koelie*, to our face. I later narrowly missed expulsion myself for shooting a water pistol at the face of my domestic science teacher, who had hurled racist abuse at me for accidentally spilling milk over her recipes. Jo admitted she was losing control of things, and agonised about our chances of ever completing our school education. Only one of us had so far made it to matric. Ami, caught up in his own world, was of no real help to her.

'I'll pay you next month, I promise you,' Jo told Savi, our neighbour from across the road, when Savi popped in that month-end to check if we had the money to pay for the vegetables we had bought on tick from her market stall over the past two months. 'I'm looking for a job with a stable income. You'll be the first one I pay once I start to earn some money.'

Always one for keeping up appearances, Ami had insisted over the years that it would be an insult to him and his family name if Jo were seen to be working for anyone outside the home. Now she had no choice but to defy him.

Not having any qualifications, with only a Standard 2 education, Jo could not find any clerical work. She had tried dressmaking in addition to door-to-door food sales in order to create a more regular income, but did not have enough customers to feed six growing children as well as cover our other basic monthly living expenses, let alone anything else.

'I've just applied for switchboard work at the Carlton Hotel,' Jo told Savi. 'The money for night shifts is good, so if I get the job I'll be able to pay you, the butcher, the grocer, and the lights and water. Please bear with me, my friend.'

She got the job.

By now Ami was a bookie who ran an illegal betting shop in a small room at the back of his unprofitable fabric shop. He was also becoming a bridge player of note, winning many South African bridge championships. The trophies he brought home covered the top of our piano. His colour, though, barred him from competing in the international Bridge Olympiad.

Still, he made news when Boris Shapiro, Britain's bridge champion, visited South Africa. Ami challenged Shapiro to a match and beat him hands down, showing the same sort of *chutzpah* Jo had found so alluring when he turned up on her convent doorstep that fateful day in 1935. Shapiro said it was a fluke and challenged him to a return round. Ami beat him hollow again.

Overnight Ami became the darling of the white bridge set that met in fancy homes in suburbs such as Northcliff and Parkview. His frustration at being among the best at professional bridge in South Africa, but not being allowed to represent his country internationally must have really got to him once he had beaten Shapiro. Now his gambling and womanising became even worse, while Jo worked hard to make ends meet in the hope of patching together the disintegrating pieces of our home and family.

The 1958 December holidays were upon us. Jo was working two shifts now. We had taken to swimming in stagnant pools on the nearby mine dumps to keep cool in the blistering heat. Public swimming pools and other such sports and recreational facilities were for whites only. In order to keep us off the streets and away from the dangerous mine dumps, Jo phoned her old friend Sam Ngoma at the Bantu Man's Social Centre near town to check if my brother Adam and I could take piano lessons with him. Sam was a brilliant jazz pianist. This was the same Mr Sam Ngoma whom Jeffrey, our domestic worker, had introduced to Jo. Jeffrey had since passed on.

During those holidays, my sister Shirene and I were also accepted for tennis lessons at the centre. This training not only gave us some-thing useful and constructive to do in the holidays, it also made our game at school stronger. And we were able to mix with Africans of our own age we would never otherwise have had the opportunity to meet socially.

Mr Ngoma even arranged that we be allowed to join the makeshift lending library at the Social Centre. Just the previous year we had been refused membership of the imposing Johannesburg Central Library because it was for whites only, at a time when our pitiful school library was the only one we had access to.

By contrast, and so tellingly, the doors of an institution intended for the use of Africans were being opened to non-Africans. Here I was experiencing, at first hand, a generosity of spirit I later came to know as *ubuntu*.

Just over a year later, Jo would donate the novels she had been buying from second-hand bookshops, to improve her command of English, to the centre. That's when I first came to know of authors such as John Steinbeck, Paul Gallico, Alexander Solzhenitshyn, Saul Bellow, Ernest Hemingway, Boris Pasternak, Irving Stone and the playwright Arthur Miller. In this pile of books for the centre Jo included her *New Age* newspapers, which she had been buying regularly from Transvaal Indian Congress activists, who were selling them door to door as part of their effort to raise the political awareness of our community.

*   *   *   *   *

'Why should I have to pay the extra rent?' Jo protested to Ami. It was one of those bombshells he sprang on her whenever she tried to stop our family from unravelling.

Mr Latib, our landlord and next-door neighbour, had just given Ami notice that, as of next month, January 1959, our rent would be raised by a third until we were relocated to Lenasia under the Group Areas Act. The Act assigned different residential areas, far outside the major cities, to Coloureds, Africans and Indians. We would soon be herded to Lenasia – but first Jo would have to pay the extra rent.

'You insist on working outside when your family needs you, so you'll have to cover any new financial needs in the home,' Ami gloated, as if to make her pay for defying his wish that she work from home, or for peanuts at his shop. 'I certainly do not have the money,' he added.

'Next thing you'll say you can't afford the monthly pittance you contribute towards food, and you'll be expecting me to pay for petrol to use your car, but I'll embarrass you again,' she hit back.

Some months earlier Jo had upset Ami terribly when some of his bridge friends had come to dinner and she served them Maltabella porridge.

'Sorry, no money for anything else,' she explained to them. She was sick and tired of pretending, something Ami managed to do with poise. He never forgave Jo for that Maltabella dinner.

Now she was once again stuck between a rock and a hard place. If Ami didn't pay the extra rent, the landlord had other prospective tenants who would. Ami could simply then go and stay with his friends or family, like he used to do in Troyeville. But it was another matter for Jo to move with her five remaining teenage children and Granny Christine from Cape Town, who had come to live with us. Mac, my eldest brother, had married and moved out. Then there was the relocation to Lenasia, which was imminent, and our school, too, was to be shut down and its buildings used as a training college for white teachers. And though the offers from Jo's friends to move in with them if things got unbearable at home were genuine, how could she impose six more of us on them? Determined not to split us up the way her mother had had to separate her sisters and brothers, Jo realised she had no choice but to pay up. Of course Ami knew all along that she would.

Then one night, Jo was dropped off at home in a staff combi that also contained some male colleagues. An argument ensued, and Ami assaulted her. Jo packed her bags and went to stay with a friend in Desai's Building, near Ferreirastown. She arranged for a woman, Sarojini, who was looking for domestic work, to live in our home and help Granny take care of us.

Some weeks later, wearing my gear for madressa – an *ijaar* to cover my legs, a long-sleeved blouse to cover my arms and a scarf to cover my head – I was just about to leave the house with my Koran wrapped in another scarf when Jo phoned me. Mariam Appa, who ran the madressa, had just called her to say she had seen me the day before with a group of Coloured boys, playing football. I had shouted as raucously as the boys, and even allowed them to hug me each time I saved a goal. This was shameful behaviour for a girl and would not be tolerated. I was, as of now, expelled from Mariam Appa's madressa!

'But Mom, I've been playing soccer since we moved here, she knows that,' I protested. 'Everybody in Fordsburg knows I play soccer after school with boys, girls, Coloureds, Indians, anybody who wants to play with me. And Adam and Doolie were the ones hugging me yesterday. So why is there suddenly a problem?'

I was genuinely puzzled. Nobody, not even my demure school friends who refused to play on Red Square – some were already into high heels, fashion and make-up – had made an issue of my soccer playing before. They just saw me as a bit of a tomboy, influenced by four older brothers, who would soon grow out of it.

'I don't know, but yes, we deserve an explanation for this decision,' was all Jo would say on the phone.

Jo had always been resilient in the face of criticism of her parenting skills, but now I could hear in her voice that it was getting to her. Like religious converts tend to do, Jo embraced her new religion. In the Muslim holy month of Ramadan, for example, she would fast as many days as she could, encouraging the rest of us to follow suit. Or she would read the English translation of the part of the Koran we were currently reading in Arabic at madressa, so that we actually understood what it said.

Although Jo could not read or write Arabic, or join in the prayers at funerals, she was very proud of my ability to do so. She always made sure, through English translations, that I understood the meaning and significance of the prayers I was chanting. Because my father had been a non-practising Muslim for some time and Jo felt it important that her children identify with a religion, she would coax us to follow her example. The festival of Eid, marking the end of Ramadan, was always celebrated at our home by Ami's extended family.

At the same time, when I visited my mother's family in Cape Town, I was made to sing hymns solo on the church stage, or lead the church choir, or recite the psalms and say grace before we ate. With Jo's family, we were not allowed to eat with our fingers, say prayers in Arabic or use running water in the toilet.

So we straddled cultures and religions, and, although both sides of the family claimed us as their own – when it suited them – we were not quite comfortable with either, especially as we got older. We did not fit into one particular box and found ourselves comparing the rituals, traditions and attitudes of the two sides. Being on the inside as outsiders could easily have led to an identity crisis were it not for the insights into insularity and prejudice that this vantage point allowed, and the many laughs we got from it.

On one occasion in Cape Town, having spent most of the day in church, I began to feel that I was letting my father's side down. So, after saying grace in Afrikaans at the supper table, I whispered the words in Arabic. My granny overheard and reprimanded me.

'You are a Christian in Cape Town,' she scolded. '*Jy's hier nie 'n Moor nie!*' ('You are no Muslim here!')

I couldn't contain my laughter at her despairing tone, as if her efforts to save my soul might be in vain. Jo too would hoot at this kind of attempt to keep us boxed in. As when I told her things I'd overheard her relatives whisper to each other, such as, '*Josie het 'n Moor getrou, en hy's wragtig swart en 'n dowwelaaar, nogal!*' ('Josie married a Muslim, he's really black and a gambler on top of it!')

Thursday nights are holy nights for Muslims, when we have to say special, long prayers. A stern uncle of mine overheard one of my brothers saying, 'Ditto as per last Thursday', to spare himself the trouble. There was hell to pay! Fortunately, some of our relatives were relaxed about this kind of thing. Still, I couldn't help noticing that even they often displayed a similar lack of tolerance towards my mother's side of the family and their traditions.

In the early fifties, Granny Christine accepted Jo's invitation to come and live with us in Joburg instead of staying in Cape Town with another of her daughters, Naomi, and son-in-law, Alec Anthony. To boot, and to our great relief, she and Ami – the 'Moor' she had so reviled – developed a better rapport than she'd ever had with any of her other in-laws. It became clear that only ignorance was reinforcing our mutual prejudices.

Granny and I shared a bedroom for seven years. For her sixtieth birthday I bought her a brand new Bible, as her old, much-used one was falling apart. I had saved up for her present from the money I got working at my uncle's shop, Abdullah's Neckwear, in Diagonal Street on Saturday mornings. With this gift, I was officially declared Granny's favourite grandchild.

Now Jo tackled Mariam Appa about why playing with the boys on Red Square was sufficient cause to expel me from madressa, and the truth came out.

'Some of your in-laws are really upset about the way you have disregarded their brother's wishes by taking on that job in the Carlton Hotel and then moving out,' Mariam Appa told Jo. 'They say you share lifts to and from work with people that include strange men. They feel you are bringing their family into disrepute, and allowing your daughters to do so too. Ami has found a wealthy husband for Zarina, but they fear at this rate he might refuse to marry her. It is your in-laws who urged me to expel her to jolt you into returning home and taking responsibility for your children.'

She then offered me back my place in her madressa.

'You can tell them I'll gladly come home and stay home if they pay me the Carlton's salary,' Jo said calmly. She stood up to leave, very upset but relieved that at least she'd got to the bottom of things. 'I'm late for work and must get back. Thanks very much for your honesty.'

*   *   *   *   *

On one occasion in 1959, my sister and I were spending a weekend with Jo at the home of her friend, Janie Abdullah, near Ferreirastown, where Jo was staying. On the Saturday morning we got a lift to Lenasia, where Indians in Johannesburg were to be relocated by law. By now the Fordsburg community had been informed that our local school, the Johannesburg Indian High, was soon to close down, and its buildings used as a training college for white teachers. Even the

University of the Witwatersrand was to become all white, except for the medical faculty, which blacks would be allowed to attend on a quota system.

The imminent forced removals, with no specific time frame, angered Jo deeply. We would be herded like cattle into a kraal, *when* it suited the authorities. There were also the practical problems: how would we afford the commuting costs between Lenasia and Johannesburg, where the jobs were? And, while we waited to be moved to Lenasia, what about the time it would take for my younger sister and me to get to Braamfontein Station and then catch the train to school, which would start at 7.30 a.m.?

Jo decided to go and see for herself how the development in Lenasia was progressing. We saw a smattering of homes going up. The site was surrounded by what looked like miles of dustbowl red sand, with little sign of any infrastructure in the vicinity. Even our future school seemed like nothing but red sand!

Jo took it all in, but said nothing.

While we were relaxing at Auntie Janie's that afternoon, there was suddenly a loud, impatient knock on her door. Auntie Janie peeped through the burglar eye and saw Ami standing outside. She tiptoed back to the sitting room and whispered to us to be quiet until he left. But the knocks grew louder and more impatient. Ami seemed to know we were inside. When Jo did not respond to his calls to be let in, he fired a shot at the lock to open it, and another for good effect, and had us trembling in our boots as he took the three of us back to Fordsburg with him.

Ami had tracked Jo down before when she was hiding from him, once even as far away as Port Elizabeth. Try as she might to get away from him, he always managed to find her. So, to give her the time and space to make her next move, she left the Carlton and took up a temporary job as a housekeeper/cook at the home of a Mrs Pohl in Houghton. The job, advertised in the 'Domestics Wanted' section of a newspaper, offered a car and self-contained accommodation, the two main reasons she applied for it. Again we visited her in secret there.

On one of these visits, Jo told me that she had just finalised the sale of her shop in Troyeville. Through the years she had managed to keep the shop solely in her maiden name, Josephine Medell, so that my father couldn't meddle in its affairs without her consent. She had quietly looked after it, first in the early days of back-breaking work to build on the shop's value, then, when she rented it out, so that it would pay off its bond.

Now, *gatvol* with an environment in which she was increasingly losing control of her own life and her children's – including our chances of ever completing school – she had finally decided to cash in her nest egg, and use this to give us a fresh start. Jo had come to the point where what she wanted most was to free us all from the tyrants in our lives – in government, and those in our family and community – who were constantly laying down the law on how we should live and conduct ourselves.

Jo figured that if we were to be uprooted from Fordsburg, we might as well go to England. Unlike the teachers and other professionals in the black community who were emigrating to places like Canada and Australia during that period, Jo could not, as none of us had a professional qualification to our name. As British subjects at the time, the requirements for our entry into England were far less stringent.

Jo broke the news to Ami of her decision to take us overseas, and quite predictably he seethed with anger, threatening to 'cut her out' of his life if she dared go ahead with such a move.

'You won't get a penny from me if you leave,' he warned Jo.

'So what's new then?' was all she said.

Granny Christine had by now also left for England. She'd saved up her wages as a garment worker in the factory next door to our house, where she had worked for much of her stay with us, after hearing that, even at her age, sixty-three, she could still get a job in England and possibly qualify for a pension.

* * * * *

When we left Johannesburg, Park Station Platform 2 was crowded with people who had come to see us off to Cape Town, where we would board the *Cape Town Castle* to England on 5 February 1960. Although both nervous and excited about making a fresh start overseas, I felt immense sadness at having to leave behind my five best friends. Very tearful at the time, I still could not have anticipated how much I would miss them, and Jozi.

Sis Rachmat, Ami and Jo's old friend, fetched us on our arrival at Cape Town Station and drove us to her house.

'That's where I hid your parents when they eloped and came to Cape Town to get married,' she said, pointing from the car to a tiny pink terraced house on Hanover Street in District Six, near central Cape Town. 'And that's where I lived with my family at the time.' She indicated a green house directly opposite, also with its front door right on the pavement. 'And that's the mosque where the Imam married your parents,' she said, and pointed to a tiny corner mosque.

Three days later we set sail. As the gangplanks were being drawn up, we waved energetically to Aunt Naomi, my mother's youngest sister, and her family, who had come to see us off. With them were Sis Rachmat and her family, and Ami, who had that morning flown into Cape Town to say goodbye. I noticed tears in Jo's eyes at the sight of Ami and Sis Rachmat together. She had been the go-between that had made their marriage possible, now she was the go-between overseeing its end.

Our cabins were two levels below deck, so small you couldn't swing a cat in them. We had two cabins, each with three bunks. These were obviously very different from the cabins above deck, one of whose occupants was Harold Macmillan, the then Prime Minister of the

UK, who had just made his 'Wind of Change' speech in parliament that week. He was referring to the growing independence of African countries from colonialist rule.

As the ship docked in Southampton harbour at 4 a.m. on a dark and icy winter morning on 19 February 1960, Jo gathered the five of us on deck – we ranged in age from thirteen to twenty. She asked that we not judge her too harshly if we ever felt it was wrong of her to have wrenched us from our roots like this.

'Rather see this place as a stepping stone to wherever else you may choose to settle down. If you decide one day you'd rather be back home,' she smiled reassuringly, 'then go back, but first you must make the most of this chance to pull yourselves up. It's the best I could offer you in the circumstances.'

CHAPTER 6

Just *do* it!

LONDON

It was nine o'clock in the morning, yet strangely as dark as midnight when we disembarked from the *Cape Town Castle* down an icy gangplank at Southampton docks. Equally strange was the sight of white porters, sweepers and other menial workers dressed in the sort of overalls only black people seemed to wear at home. Their accents were so foreign, we could not always understand what they were saying. As we cleared customs and passport control, we came face to face with the large crowd who'd come to meet the other passengers we'd travelled with. There was not a sinner in the world to greet us.

If anything brought home to Jo the fact that we were now truly on our own in an alien land, it was this. Not that we had expected anyone. Granny Christine was at work as a housekeeper/maid for a disabled Polish widow in Fulham and never got a weekday off. In any case, it was too long a train trip from London at her age, and also too expensive.

Feeling suddenly forlorn in such a strange setting with nothing familiar to latch onto, Jo panicked for a moment and began rummaging through her handbag to make sure the traveller's cheques – bought out of what was left from the sale of her Troyeville shop after paying our passage to England and our debts in Fordsburg – were still safely there. Although not much, it would keep us going till Jo and my brothers found work, and we found our feet. At that moment Jo realised that she could no longer indulge her apprehensions about her decision to bring us to England. Now that we were in at the deep end, it was either sink or swim.

Anxious to see what this England, with its promises of freedom, hope and opportunity looked like, I scrambled for a window seat on the train to London's Victoria Station. The undulating snowy white fields with ice-covered bare branches looked as beautiful as a Christmas card. What I wasn't prepared for, though, was the sameness of all the houses on the railway track in nearly every town. Unlike our homes in Fordsburg, Fietas and Ferreirastown – considered slums by many – these neatly identical terraced houses had no character at all! But what surprised me more was that they seemed so modest for white people. I'd imagined they mostly lived like they did in Parkview, Houghton and Northcliff, in distinctive homes with beautiful gardens, swimming pools and maid's quarters, like the Pohls' home, where Jo had recently worked. These terraced houses – I later learnt they were built at very low cost after the Second World War from just one architectural plan per row of terraces – compounded my utter surprise earlier when, for the first time, I'd seen white people on their hands and knees cleaning toilets, scrubbing floors and carrying our baggage!

Another enduring first impression of my adopted country on that trip to London was the way the pitch-black morning sky later turned a dark grey that seemed to match everything, including the regimented houses. That grey came to signify for me the overwhelming colour of life itself in England.

*   *   *   *   *

The next morning we travelled on a red double-decker bus from the bed and breakfast near Victoria Station, where we had spent our first night, to an adjacent residential area called Pimlico, where there was a flat to let at four pounds ten shillings, the cheapest advertised in the early-morning newspapers.

What a dump it was! Dark, dank, cold and musty, it was a basement flat consisting of two tiny rooms and a kitchen, each to the left off a narrow passage that started at the front door – accessible from the pavement via a steep and dangerous ice-covered concrete staircase – and ended at the back door, through which the only toilet, in equally bad condition, could be reached outside.

There was no bathroom. Though we were badly put off by the place, Jo grabbed it because it was a cheap roof over our heads and immediately available. Jo felt that with a bit of elbow grease, a lick of paint and some tender loving care, we could quickly transform the flat. When we again complained about the lack of a bathroom on the way back to the bed and breakfast to fetch our suitcases, Jo explained that the basin in the toilet could be filled with water, which could be scooped up using a jug, to have an Indian-style bath.

'Or we could go to the public baths, as the maids and other staff once did who used to occupy the staff quarters of these Victorian homes,' she tried to console us. 'The landlord says the public baths are a twenty-five-minute walk from here.'

The matter was thereby closed for discussion.

That afternoon we moved in.

I prayed like anything that night: that my dad would come to his senses, that my family would find work quickly so that we'd not have to worry so much about making ends meet, that my brothers would be able to go back to school one day, that Jo would make new friends and get a bit of a life for herself, that we'd swim instead of sink in the deep end. What if Jo was to die suddenly? This thought frightened me again, as it often had in Fordsburg.

A week later, Jo returned home one afternoon after making a few telephone calls at the local public phone box in response to job advertisements she'd seen in the papers that morning. She asked me nervously, 'Zarina, what's a negative number? They say at the interview tomorrow I'll need to demonstrate my understanding of negative numbers to be considered for the job. You've got to help me!'

I spent that afternoon explaining what -2 means as opposed to $+2$, in terms of *owing* two eggs as opposed to *owning* them, and the arithmetic rules of negative numbers. Though Jo had actually been using the concept of a negative number to balance the books of her Troyeville business, she never realised this. Next day she had the interview, but she would only hear whether she had the job in another week.

While Jo waited, she arranged for the London County Council to assess my sister and me for school placing. On this basis they recommended the most suitable local schools, which we began attending the following week, just two weeks after our arrival in London.

'I've got the job as a clerk at Unilever, at their central London branch!' Jo said and hugged me joyously on the first day I attended school in England. At ten pounds ten shillings a week, we were not complaining.

Within another week, Adam, the youngest of the brothers – and the unshakeable rock of our family through that trying period so far from home – found a job in a legal firm as a junior apprentice at four pounds ten a week, exactly what we were paying for rent.

Just a week after Adam started working, on 21 March 1960, the Sharpeville massacre took place in South Africa. Sixty-nine unarmed men and women, peacefully protesting apartheid pass laws, were shot and killed in cold blood by the South African police, resulting in the watershed decision of the ANC leadership in December of the following year to launch the armed liberation struggle.

So thoroughly did BBC radio and television reveal the barbarity of the Sharpeville massacre, its aftermath, and the historic and economic rationale for the pass laws underpinning apartheid segregation, it was something of an education in itself. It shocked us into realising just how far the brutal regime would go to maintain white privilege.

Soon afterwards, Enver, my brother who had attended university in South Africa as an occasional student, also got a job, at Dunlop, as a clerk earning nine pounds a week. Only Doolie was unlucky for a year, partly because he was very nervous of white people and therefore afraid of interviews. He was even nervous about boarding 'white' buses and sitting next to white passengers. When he did muster the courage to go to interviews, his lack of confidence showed.

Doolie must have been one of the very first hippies of sixties' London, with his mane of long hair, which he grew simply because he was apprehensive of the white barbers who might refuse to cut his hair because of the colour of his skin!

Despite these three incomes, Jo was forced to find a second job, as they didn't cover our living expenses. After knocking off from Unilever at 5 p.m., she would take the tube to Knightsbridge to look after a wealthy Australian family. She would cook their dinner, set the table, serve their food, then clean up afterwards and draw up a list of ingredients for the following evening's meal.

During this period Jo never got home before midnight during the week. Spurred on by the prospect that another job would allow her to move us to a bigger, better flat, with an inside bathroom, she also took on a weekend job at the Playboy Club in Park Lane, opposite Hyde Park – not, of course, as a Playboy Bunny, but as a coatroom attendant. The famous celebrities who frequented the club, and whose furs, hats and umbrellas she looked after, tipped her extravagantly.

Through sheer grit, Jo was beginning to pull us all up by her bootstraps, almost relishing the challenge despite her sheer exhaustion and melancholy at times. But she was always conscious of the example she was setting. Every four or five months, when her responsibilities started overwhelming her, she would get a sick note from her doctor to take three or four days off work to recharge her batteries. Then she would return to her three jobs, with no time to relax in between. She was totally driven and focused on her need to give her children a better education and life than she'd had. And she was determined to succeed in her goal without the support of my father or anyone else.

'We're really in at the deep end. We have to keep swimming hard to keep from sinking. And there's no free lunch in this world, so just *do* it,' she would tell us off impatiently whenever we cried or complained about having been wrenched so painfully from our roots and about the harshness of life in London, a place that often seemed like the armpit of the universe, damp and sunless as it was – as well as expensive, aloof and unfriendly.

But with Jo's unstinting support we pushed on, and things started looking up. In July 1961, I obtained the British equivalent of the South African matric, the General Certificate of Education Ordinary Level, with distinction; one of my brothers, Enver, resumed his studies at evening classes in September of that year; Jo was promoted at Unilever to administrative head of the personnel department.

As English was not her mother tongue, Jo now started taking English grammar lessons to improve her command of the language. As she had done on her night shifts at the Carlton in Johannesburg, she read novels whenever she had the time, at first to expand her vocabulary and later because reading became a passion.

I also landed my first holiday job, having traipsed from door to door, asking shops and offices in the city of Westminster for work for days on end. It was fun earning my own money as an architect's messenger, tasked that summer with hand-delivering his plans to his clients in every nook and cranny of London. Best of all, though, was when we moved into a light and airy first-floor, three-bedroom flat in Camberwell Green, South London, just before Christmas 1962. The flat overlooked a communal garden, to which all the tenants had access, and we could finally unpack the trunks filled with our household goods from Fordsburg.

One Saturday afternoon sometime in early 1963, I had just finished my weekend house-cleaning chores when there was a knock at the door. When I opened it, the person introduced himself as Laloo Chiba. He had arrived from South Africa a couple of days earlier, and had now come to visit his youngest brother Chips, then a lodger in our home, who had a year before come to study Aeronautical Engineering at the University of London.

Although none of us knew it at the time, Laloo was a high-ranking member of the ANC's military wing, Umkhonto we Sizwe (or MK), meaning 'Spear of the Nation'. He was passing through London on his way to the Soviet Union for training. He and I got on so well that, when he was imprisoned for twenty years on Robben Island for his MK sabotage activities in 1964, I started writing to him – a correspondence that unwittingly introduced me to his co-prisoner Mac Maharaj, serving twelve years on Robben Island for 177 counts of sabotage as an MK commander.

Mac apparently read all my letters to Laloo, and in this way got to know me well during his imprisonment. If I'd had any idea that my letters were being read by other prisoners, I am sure I would have said less about myself and been less forthright. In any case, Mac secured something of an advantage over me through my letters to Laloo: he got to know me before he even met me, at a time when I'd only heard about him.

Just before the period of this correspondence, I had worked as a waitress by day and studied at night for my university entrance qualifications. I also hitch-hiked in Europe or Britain on working holidays whenever I could. I eventually left home when I could no longer put up with an abusive and obnoxious brother who railed, among other things, at my relationship with Chips, once his friend and now my boyfriend, 'but' a Hindu. Chips moved out.

When I told Jo I would be leaving too, she took me to see an old family friend from South Africa, Dr Enver Cassim Adam, who had also settled in London. He was an ardent bridge player, and had introduced my parents to his colleague and friend, Doctor Rex, an African bridge player of note, who also became a family friend.

Now Jo offered some of her jewellery to Dr Adam in exchange for a monthly loan, which would supplement the paltry wages I earned as a waitress. It would allow me to pay the rent on the tiny bedsitter I'd found in Victoria, near the government-owned Westminster College of Further Education that I was attending. My books I would continue to fund from my waitressing work.

Dr Adam refused to accept the collateral, but agreed to the loan on condition that I repay him once I graduated. He was extremely pleased when I paid him back in full on completion of my studies a few years later. I am friends with Dr Adam's daughter, Duria, to this day.

That's how I managed to complete my university entrance studies in 1965/66. I was then able to gain admission to a university fairly close to Chips's new job, way up in the Midlands at Rolls-Royce in Derby. Then, to the sheer horror of my father's sister, who had come to live in London, but with Jo's full blessing, I married Chips, across religious lines.

'It's as bad as an Arab marrying a Jew,' my aunt Hanifa objected vehemently. So I didn't invite her to my wedding.

By now I had started visiting the recently established ANC office in London and participating in the movement's fundraising activities, in this way getting to know the functionaries. So, by 1966 I had lots to write about to Laloo, some of it by innuendo to escape the censor's pen. A narrow, rickety staircase led up to the first-floor office. Made up of just two small, threadbare rooms sharing a desk, a few chairs and a filing cabinet, the office was housed in a shabby little building in St Ann's Court, Soho, in the heart of London's West End.

I would pop in to greet Reg September, the ANC's chief representative in London, whenever I was in that part of town. '*Slamse meisiekind* [Muslim girl-child],' he would greet me endearingly. I never figured out why my religion was so much a part of his perception of me, as I had long ago stopped being religious, especially after my expulsion from madressa. In fact, I had by then already begun to question the existence of God.

It was through Billy Nannan, a political exile now settled in London and an old school friend of Chips's and one of my brothers, that we began to meet people like Thabo Mbeki and his friends Essop and Aziz Pahad, whom many referred to as 'two Ps in the Pod' because of their membership of a small, closed group in the London ANC. We would meet socially at dinners and parties in the homes of Billy, Percy Cohen, Wolfie Kodesh, the Pahads, Pallo Jordan, Cab Zungu, Godfrey Motsepe, Alex La Guma, Paul Joseph, Ramni Naidoo, Dulcie September and several other political exiles and anti-apartheid activists.

Such get-togethers continued fairly regularly after our return to London from the Midlands in 1970, when General Electric offered me the position of mathematician in their telecommunications department at their research centre in Wembley. I was then able to start attending ANC youth meetings and study groups at weekends, where participants would contribute discussion papers, in rotation, on topical South African issues, something I found stimulating and exciting, and which demanded a fair amount of research effort.

And I was now also able to join the team headed by Gill Marcus, later Deputy Minister of Finance and Deputy Governor of the Reserve Bank of South Africa, who produced the first ANC weekly news briefings, which she circulated to ANC missions around the world. Reg September also commandeered me to address an occasional meeting in different parts of Britain to talk about ANC history and policy, sometimes going as far afield as Wales and Scotland.

The Anti-Apartheid Movement of Britain, working closely with the ANC, would often draw on voluntary support for its office work, and for the vigils, demonstrations and marches it organised to raise awareness among the public, and to protest against Britain's investments in South Africa and ongoing human rights abuses in the country. When I could, I would participate here too.

Even so, it seemed that unless you belonged to the South African

Communist Party – and certainly if you were bold enough to question its paradigm of the world – you were treated with arrogance and wariness by the ANC inner circle in London, a ruling clique of mainly Stalinist types who did not hesitate to use their authority in the movement against those perceived as 'ideologically naive' or independent-minded. At best we were 'bourgeois', at worst, dangerous.

The most blinkered, self-righteous and holier-than-thou types in this clique were those who had dogmatised Marxist ideology. In the mid-seventies, I once asked a leading member of the South African Communist Party, who lived in London, to explain why he saw the Marxist theory of history and society as the undisputed 'winning horse in the race of social theories'. He sternly rebuked me: 'It is the *only* horse in the race!'

This shocked me, coming from so senior a person, as his retort simply closed off any debate about the validity of other paradigms for understanding society and the world. It was as if one specific set of ideological values – and the concepts, theories, perceptions, and social, economic and political findings based on them – added up to the only 'real' truths about the world.

I had just read *The Structure of Scientific Revolutions* by TS Kuhn. In that book, the author explains that human knowledge, both in the way that it is produced and the view of the social world that it constructs, is always driven by political or technical interests and values. Such values are therefore part of the content of our understanding of the world; they determine and infuse the 'facts' we know about it.

Scientists, Kuhn explains, discover facts (or 'truths') about the world through a 'paradigm of knowledge production' that is a specific 'constellation of values, beliefs and perceptions of reality, which together with a body of theory based on the foregoing, is used by a group of scientists, and by applying a distinctive methodology, to interpret some aspect of the universe we inhabit'. In this sense, any 'scientific' truth about the world is value-laden – it is a group of scientists' interpretation of the world.

There can therefore be as many truths about 'an aspect of our universe' as there are scientists with different values and interests.

This theory was not new. Certain scientists and philosophers had held this view as far back as the nineteenth century. In challenging 'bourgeois' philosophy and science, this view was implicit in Marxist theory itself. Yet my 'one-horse-race' friend would not retract. He, and others like him, insisted that the 'real' or 'objective' truths about the social world could only be revealed in theories consistent with Marx's overarching thesis of historical materialism. The two post-modern feminist philosophers, Nancy Fraser and Linda Nicholson, recently encapsulated the essence of this thesis as 'the forward march of human productive capacities via class conflict culminating in proletarian revolution'.

Scarily, others like my one-horse-race friend had appointed themselves owners-in-exile of the South African revolution. They saw themselves as the 'true' revolutionaries of the struggle at home, members of some sort of exclusive club, labelling and marginalising as 'apolitical', even 'unpatriotic', those who would not toe their line. As if there can be a monopoly on patriotism!

It would have made my life so much easier if I had simply accepted that the world was heading for a proletarian revolution. I wished I could believe the one-horse theorist. I *wanted* to be guided by a paradigm, a worldview, that resonated with me both emotionally – and Marxism/Leninism did so at the time, as it did for many members of the liberation movement – and rationally. But in the absence of persuasive argument, I couldn't. These theories were often dished out as take-it-or-leave-it mantras, especially by those who used them as a crutch.

Marxism had claimed to be able to explain everyone's economic, social and political experiences in terms of the historically unfolding class conflict between capital and labour. But in 1975, the eminent social anthropologist Gayle Rubin, in her quest to understand the power relationships that subordinate women to men, exposed a serious deficiency in this theory when she showed its inability to explain, from its class-based perspective, the experiences of oppressed women in societies. Nor could Marxist theory recommend a feminist political strategy for changing such oppression: in their view, the overthrow of capitalism by the working class would automatically liberate women. Rubin wrote then: 'If sexism is a by-product of capitalism's relentless appetite for profit, then sexism would wither away in the advent of a socialist revolution.'

And it was not only the experiences of women that could not be explained in terms of class conflict, but also those whose oppression could not be reduced to economics, like sexual minorities. Suddenly, around the end of 1976, the one-horse-race theorist invited me to start attending Marxist classes. But my questions persisted even after those lessons. Luckily for me, I continued to work mostly with the less bullying, less sectarian, less judgemental among the comrades.

My avid reading during this period only served to reinforce one question: If there could be as many truths as there were theorists with different ideological standpoints or perspectives based on culture and experience, then whose truth counted as the 'real', the 'objective' truth? *Someone's* must if we are not to abandon the idea of universally accepted truths that transcend specific perspectives and that make up the established body of knowledge of the social and natural sciences. This question was in fact to become a central focus of feminist philosophers of science, such as Sandra Harding and Susan Hekman, in the mid-eighties.

It was early in 1990, during my time at the Institute of Development Studies at Sussex University, while Mac was underground in South Africa, that I gained access to the insights and debates that provided me with an answer to this question.

These insights, particularly those of the so-called Third Wave of feminists, which started in the mid-eighties, had culminated in the articulation of a new 'post-feminist' paradigm of knowledge production, the so-called 'fusion of horizons'. Scientists operating this new paradigm would produce a new, more inclusive body of 'post-feminist' social science, based on the experience of diverse social groups, than had hitherto been accepted in the male-dominated academy.

To be admitted as truth in this new science, the findings of men and women, black and white, rich and poor, straight and gay, from the developing and developed world – infused with very different values and perspectives – would be publicly scrutinised, debated and criticised by a community of established scientists in the relevant field, to see if they satisfied the following criteria of 'objective' or 'scientific' truth: the quality of evidence marshalled in support of the claim; the validity of the reasoning involved; and the consistency of the finding with what has already been established truth in the field.

'Objectivity' denied or conferred on a value-laden claim to truth, through this process of 'intersubjective verification', is at the heart of the new post-feminist science. It is through this concept of value-laden objectivity that the scientific findings of feminists have, for example, gained academic legitimacy and are being incorporated into the body of established social science, whereas previously their findings were relegated to separate 'women's studies' courses – or not acknowledged in the academy at all.

Here now was a paradigm of knowledge production that genuine scientists, of whatever political persuasion or social grouping, could embrace. Scientific research that meets its criteria of objectivity – and which therefore produces generally accepted truths about women, blacks, workers, the poorest of the poor or sexual minorities – has the power to influence policy and legislation and to change belief systems about these social groups. In this sense, scientific research is a terrain of struggle, whether for the New Left, for women, or for groups seeking a voice.

At the same time, this paradigm has rendered obsolete the Marxist monopoly on truth, which effectively 'banned independent thought', to quote Václav Havel, the Czech poet who later became Czechoslovakia's first post-communist president.

It threw down the gauntlet to those London-based bigots who had so readily invoked dogma as a weapon and a crutch. Many of them, following the fall of communism in the nineties, too easily and conveniently discarded the dogma, though not necessarily their resentment of independent thinking.

It became evident to me that one's acceptance in the 'struggle family', and one's position and the treatment one could expect in the pecking order of ANC activists, depended on a clear set of factors. These included whether you were a member of the Communist Party, or at least idealised it; whether you had been an activist or imprisoned in South Africa before arriving in Britain; whether you were part of a high-profile family from home, political or otherwise, or connected with a family who had contributed to the ANC financially; whether you were a draft dodger; and whether, if you were at the bottom of this order because you met none of these criteria – even if you were competent and completely committed – you were nevertheless willing and ready to brown-nose your way up. You could, for example, comply with unashamed requests – by a few in the inner circle – for your 'services', which were unrelated to political work, especially if you were an attractive woman.

When I was twenty-one years old, I attended a party with ANC exiles at the North London home of Percy Cohen, a dentist and member of the movement. A young, leading member of the ANC, who was about my age, approached me with the memorable line: 'Prove you are not a racist by sleeping with me'!

All he scored that night were some points for originality. I've never taken kindly to emotional blackmail! But I later came to learn that this line, though playing the race card, was actually quite effective with some women.

The fewer of these criteria you met, the further down the pecking order you were and the more patronising the treatment you received, regardless of what you were able to offer the movement in terms of dedication and skills, both of which only counted if you conformed and toed the line. Never an ideologue for the sake of it, and always conscious of my right to differ, I was definitely never going to make it up the order, that was becoming clear.

In the mid-seventies, when I asked how I could be of more use, I was told that the movement would be able to deploy me 'after liberation and during social reconstruction', given my specialised skills. And, young as I was then, raring to get more directly involved in struggle work, I came to realise that my only chance of drawing closer to the real action would be to escape the stranglehold of the leadership clique in the exile circle in London.

In 1975, Billy Nannan, who'd heard me sing in a student jazz group at university, asked me to join Mayibuye, the cultural unit of the ANC in London. Through song and poetry we were to take the message of the South African struggle to the British people. The unit performed so well that we were invited to Europe, where we became a hit, and were asked to return to perform many times. We even cut a disc.

Reg September was so impressed with the success of our performances, mobilising British and European public opinion against the apartheid regime, that he seriously suggested we turn professional. The ANC would pay us for our work, and we would do it full time rather than just at weekends. But there was not enough money for that, and the idea was dropped.

We must indeed have had some impact, or else apartheid agents working in Europe at the time would not have reported our activities. Even Afrikaans newspapers such as *Rapport* were carrying reports about Mayibuye's work in Europe after the 1976 Soweto Uprising. They even named us individually: Barry Feinberg, Pallo Jordan, John Matshikiza, Billy Nannan, Ronnie Kasrils, Bongi Dhlomo, Melody Mthetwa, Godfrey Motsepe and me. Others came later. This may explain why, when I applied for a visa for a second time to enter South Africa on a British passport, I was again refused. I had wanted to visit Laloo Chiba on Robben Island.

In early 1973, while still working at General Electric, I had reluctantly turned down a position as lecturer in mathematics at the University of Algiers. I was concerned about reports on how single foreign women were treated in Algeria, especially now that I would be on my own – Chips and I had agreed to separate.

Soon after that, Jo, who lived with me, was diagnosed with inoperable ovarian cancer and given six weeks to live. The news devastated me. I could not face losing her. At fifty-nine, she was still working at Unilever – but had now left the Playboy Club and had stopped doing housekeeping work – and had just learnt to ski while holidaying in Switzerland over the past Christmas break with my sister and her French husband.

On a summer holiday some two years before, she had similarly opted for something altogether different and new, hitch-hiking with her eldest grandson Xavier through Italy, happily accepting lifts on horse carts and even tractors to get them to their destinations. She finally reached Florence, where she realised one of her life's goals: to see Michelangelo's astonishing David, his tribute to the man who had defeated Goliath.

Before that, in Rome, she had seen Michelangelo's ceiling paintings in the Sistine Chapel in the Vatican. As she absorbed the beauty of the work, she tried to imagine the pain he had endured when the paint dripped from the ceiling into his eyes as he battled to finish the task. It was a difficult period in his life, vividly described in the biographical novel, *The Agony and the Ecstasy*, by Irving Stone.

Jo also saw Michelangelo's astonishing Pietà in St Peter's Basilica. She had come to love the artist passionately, and talked about him as if he were still alive!

With all her vivacity and lust for life, I was suddenly told she had just six weeks left to live. I pulled out all the stops, with her doctor's support and guidance, to try to extend those six weeks. Her sheer will to live eventually gave her another two years. During this time, and despite the severity of her illness and the chemotherapy treatment, she responded to my father's pleas for her to come and nurse him at his sister's home in London, where he had been living, on and off, since his arrival in England in the mid-sixties.

Now that hope of his recovery from prostrate cancer had faded, Ami was discharged from hospital to go home to die. Jo's selfless sacrifice reflected the same generosity of spirit she had shown towards Ami three years earlier, when she had agreed to take him back after he had pleaded for another chance. Perhaps it was Jo's determination to pick up the pieces and put them back together; perhaps she just enjoyed Ami's sharp wit; perhaps it was simply a forgiveness that comes with age. But whatever her reasons for taking him back, Ami had blown even that last chance.

Still, Jo nursed him compassionately until the moment of his death, seeing at first hand how cancer withers you to the bone. She witnessed the different stages of approaching death she herself would have to go through. Only after Ami's death did Jo go ahead and visit my siblings – as far afield as France, Germany, Ethiopia and Canada – who had sent for her on learning that she was terminally ill.

Jo used this opportunity to bid them goodbye by giving them each a small keepsake from her favourite possessions. There was an antique Indian brass mortar and pestle, her books, a ruby ring my father had worn, a few European and Indian period furniture pieces she had bought at auctions, and an original painting by an unknown artist that she loved. She left her youngest son Adam, who deserved it most for steadfastly carrying our family in our most trying years, her paid-up insurance policy.

But it was Jo's values, and the boldness with which she lived by them, that were her real legacy to us. I feel blessed to this day that she died in my arms.

Jo remained a faithful Muslim up to her death, explaining to me right to the end how I should carry out the relevant Muslim rituals, including which shops in London's East End stocked the calico in which her corpse was to be wrapped in accordance with Muslim burial rites. There were even handwritten notes in her wardrobe, in case she did not make it home, with instructions on how to do everything correctly during the funeral procedures. The notes also encouraged me to be strong and thanked me for staying by her side throughout.

We had neither of us shied away from openly discussing her imminent death, which she faced as courageously as she had faced her difficult life. Her oncologist, Mr Simmons, called me in September 1974, soon after Jo had passed away, to tell me that of all the cancer patients he had treated through the years, there were three he would never forget for their wonderful humour, dignity and resolute calm in the face of death: John Nash, the renowned British artist; Richard Dimbleby, the renowned journalist; and Jo, the unknown mother.

Among the notes I later found in her wardrobe was a poem, copied in her handwriting, by her favourite poet Rainer Maria Rilke, starting with the line 'The panther of death, swiftly it is welcome ...'

*   *   *   *   *

It was now late 1976. Following Jo's death I had moved on from General Electric to a job at the Xerox Research Laboratories in Hertfordshire. 'Professionals committed to the development and growth of Mozambique, we need you', the advertisement in the *African Communist*, a quarterly journal of the South African Communist

Party, declared. I occasionally read the journal for reference purposes, as when my turn was nearing to present a paper to one of the Saturday ANC Youth League meetings on South Africa's black middle class.

MAGIC, the Mozambique, Angola and Guinea Bissau Information Centre, a body representing the governments of these countries in London, had placed the ad. It also acted as their vetting and recruitment agency.

Mozambique had won its independence the year before, in 1975, under the leadership of FRELIMO, and already there was a mass exodus to Portugal and South Africa of Mozambican and Portuguese teachers, doctors, engineers, nurses, civil servants, bureaucrats, business people and those with other skills. I was excited by the prospect that, if my application for a job in Mozambique were to succeed, this would be a real opportunity to use my talents where I'd always wanted, in the struggle for social justice. I immediately called MAGIC to make enquiries, especially as this move would also bring me a step closer to home.

After several interviews by representatives of the Mozambican government to assess both my technical and political suitability for work in that country, I was told my application would be submitted to the relevant government department in Mozambique on condition of an ANC security clearance. The ANC's chief representative granted this.

Then, in May 1977, I received a telegram from a Professor Beirao, a FRELIMO stalwart who headed the Faculty of Mathematics at Eduardo Mondlane University in Maputo, offering me the position of lecturer in mathematics and computer science in his department. He asked me to start as soon as possible. I was offered this position despite my request to work in a rural school, far outside the city.

On hearing about the offer, my colleagues at Xerox were taken aback to learn that I'd even been considering this move. In their minds, I was not thinking clearly.

'Are you having a nervous breakdown or something?' they asked. 'Your career with Xerox is just beginning to take off and you want to go to that backwater?' was their general attitude.

Some months earlier, I had presented my findings on relevant index processing methods to the vice-president of Xerox International, who had come to the UK from the USA to be briefed on our work, at the Xerox Research Laboratories in Hertfordshire. This was part of our team's research into the prototype of the fax machine, then called a 'communicating photocopier'.

Following the presentation, the US team offered me a position as head of a research unit at Xerox's laboratories in Palo Alto, California. While the move was being arranged, I was transferred from the Hertfordshire laboratories to Xerox's UK headquarters in Euston, London, to broaden my experience in preparation for Palo Alto. Here one of my colleagues was Humphrey Tizard, grandson of Sir Henry Tizard, the celebrated scientist who, during the years from the late twenties to 1942, became an outstanding authority on aeronautics and the development of radar.

Humphrey, like my other colleagues, could not fathom why I would go to Mozambique instead of Palo Alto, especially as my perks in the US were to include an apartment, a car and annual return tickets to London. They suggested I take a break and reconsider my decision.

The truth is that, having been wined and dined by some of the top Dior and Cardin suits at Xerox, and having become familiar with their views and attitudes on women and the world, I feared that the move to Palo Alto, significant as it might be for enhancing my career in such forward-looking scientific research, could easily suck me into a milieu that was too far removed in ethos, values and distance from the revolutionary new world that was now so accessible, and so much closer to my heart.

So I thanked them for all their support, encouragement and the opportunity to learn so much, and handed in my notice in early 1977.

Now, after seventeen long years away, I would finally be taking my first step homeward.

It was about 7 p.m. on Friday 8 August, the eve of South Africa's Women's Day, when I answered the phone to a resonant voice introducing himself as Mac Maharaj, who had just that morning arrived in the UK from South Africa.

'I have a message for you and Chips from Laloo,' he said. It turned out we would be at the same venue the next day to celebrate Women's Day.

By the time I reached the venue, Mac was already seated with another Robben Islander who had just arrived in the country with him, Indres Naidoo. Hilda Bernstein, a leading struggle figure, chaired the meeting. She stood up, opened the meeting, and welcomed and introduced the men to the audience. Hilda was extremely emotional in her welcome, reminiscing fondly about how she and Mac had worked together before his arrest, and sketching out the course of events that had led to his and Indres's jailing in 1964.

Sensitively, she did not dwell on the details of the severe torture Mac had suffered in detention. Instead, she quoted news reports at the time of his trial in 1964, which described him as the 'most tortured political detainee in South Africa'. She also referred the audience to a book on South Africa's political prisoners, which, she said, included some details of the 'sadistic and obscene' torture Mac had undergone. I wasn't sure what long-serving ex-prisoners who had been tortured were supposed to look like, but here was one who'd clearly not been beaten down.

On the contrary, the harsh conditions and hard labour in the blinding sunlight of Robben Island's lime quarry seemed to have made Mac lean and fit, giving him a bronzed, healthy-looking complexion. His gleaming white smile also belied the suffering he had endured.

But what struck me most about Mac that day was the humility of his response when Hilda described him as a hero of the struggle.

'We are heroes only because we happened to be caught,' Mac said. 'There are thousands whose work in the struggle at home continues unrecognised, who carry on clandestinely, risking life and limb in the fulfilment of their difficult tasks. They are the real heroes of the struggle whom we should not forget. Let us honour them today,' he urged so emotionally that the audience spontaneously burst into songs of praise for all our freedom fighters.

Once he had briefed us about the situation at home, the celebrations started officially. We sang and recited poetry. During the serving of refreshments, Mac was able to mingle and meet some of the crowd. I had no idea then that he already knew a lot about me from my letters to his co-prisoner Laloo, Chips's brother. But before Mac could convey Laloo's message to us, the media arrived to interview him and Indres about life and the conditions on Robben Island. The throngs around them made it unlikely that we would get a chance to speak to Mac that day, so we decided to meet him another time, and went home.

By now I had confirmed my acceptance of Professor Beirao's offer at Universidade Eduardo Mondlane, booked my flight to Mozambique and had immersed myself in learning to speak Portuguese. Fluency in the language was just one of my priorities. Another was to design my maths courses using feedback on what and how my prospective students had already been taught. Then I had to attend the various MAGIC induction courses aimed at helping us to understand the new emerging revolutionary culture, and alerting us to the difficulties that could occur even in the cities, such as unclean drinking water, malaria, and the unavailability of basic medicines and even women's tampons!

Chips, who was now working at Rolls-Royce London, would not be joining me. Though we had long agreed to separate, we had remained good friends. Throughout Jo's long illness he had continued being like a son to her, and, following her death, when I was grief-stricken and inconsolable at having lost her, he was my pillar of strength.

A compassionate and gentle, self-effacing soul from the time I married him in late 1965, Chips preferred to avoid political personalities and spent most of his free time working on his sculptures, drawings and engineering designs. These were rated so highly at the Harrow College of Technology and Art, where he attended evening classes, that, though the work of an unknown amateur, they were always snapped up at exhibitions.

This gift, to visualise even the most complex objects three-dimensionally, is what made Chips so successful in his work as an aeronautical engineer in the team that designed one of Rolls-Royce's most popular and better-known jet engines, the RB.211. While his brother Laloo, who had put him through university, was in jail, Chips made sure that he sent a portion of his salary to Laloo's wife and children every month to help support them. A real *mensch*; sadly we were just not like-minded enough on too many issues.

During this hectic and exciting time, while I was preparing for the new experience of Mozambique, Chips and I saw Mac a few times. It was years later that I learnt Mac had spent six months of this period working on the manuscript of Madiba's autobiography *Long Walk to Freedom*, which he had smuggled out of prison. The London rumour mill, swirling at full speed as always, claimed that Mac was to be based in Lusaka, at ANC headquarters, once he left London, and that his wife Tim, who had moved to England and settled there during his imprisonment on Robben Island, might not be joining him.

On the eve of my departure for Mozambique, an old Fordsburg flame of Chips's, Farida Dollie, turned up at our flat seeking accommodation. She had just arrived from Beirut in Lebanon, where she had been teaching at the university. The fighting in Lebanon between Syrian and Lebanese forces, and between groups backing Palestinians and Israelis respectively, had intensified to the point where expatriates in Beirut were leaving in droves. A month before, we had cleared Farida's MG sports car, which she had sent on in advance of her arrival, at customs at Heathrow Airport.

Farida and Chips were clearly thrilled to see each other again, and they drove me to the airport on the day of my departure. We bumped into my brother Enver, whom I hadn't seen for years, and who was more overwhelmed to meet Farida than me: she had, after all, been one of Fordsburg's *femmes fatales* in the fifties. Enver was with his English wife, seeing off someone else.

Enver's talent as a writer and his predilection for cannabis, which had threatened to destroy his potential during his troubled teens in Fordsburg, had been among the reasons Jo had decided to uproot us all and take us to England. Here Enver's writing blossomed. Without question one of Jo's favourite children, she had believed in him totally, always looking out for him, right up to the moment of her death.

When Enver spotted me at the airport with a knapsack of books on my back, he seemed astounded that I was journeying to a destination still reeling from a war of liberation, and totally on my own as well! It was no big deal, I assured him. After all, upping and going was precisely what our late mother had done when her circumstances had become too stifling and the attitudes in her circle too constraining.

Under the carping and disparaging eye of a clique of zealots in Fordsburg, her space to grow and develop had steadily shrunk, as had mine in London. Our history of being at odds with convention, of dancing to a different rhythm, was repeating itself, a case of déjà vu if ever there was one!

As I boarded the aeroplane for Lisbon, Portugal, to connect with a flight to Mozambique, another stepping stone homewards, I couldn't believe my luck!

PART III

And Then There was Light

CHAPTER 7

And fullness in life became a flood

MAPUTO

'Where is your work permit from the university, or some other official clearance to allow you to take up employment here?' the handsome young immigration official at passport control asked me politely as he glanced through my passport and the university's letter of appointment.

'Professor Beirao of the Faculdade de Matemática of the Universidade Eduardo Mondlane is meeting me here this morning and would have brought the necessary documents with him,' I responded confidently, parroting Beirao's promise about immigration matters in his most recent communication with me.

'He should have lodged those documents by now,' the passport official replied, calmly motioning me to an office behind his desk, where he asked me to wait while he attended to the rest of the passengers who had also just disembarked at Maputo airport. Exhausted from the long journey from London via Lisbon and Johannesburg, and from weeks of preparing and packing to settle in Maputo for at least the duration of my two-year contract, I collapsed into a small, broken-down armchair in a corner of the tiny office. Here was an unexpected break in my trip I could use well until Beirao came to my rescue with the necessary papers.

I passed out in the armchair. When the passport guy eventually came to see me, it was already 10.30 a.m. I had arrived at 8.00 a.m. 'Professor Beirao has still not arrived. I will phone him at the faculty to remind him you are here,' he said, as he kindly gave me a cup of coffee.

I went looking for a bathroom. The walls of the arrivals hall were adorned with the new Mozambican flag and pictures of President Samora Machel, who'd been in the vanguard of those who'd led the Mozambican liberation movement to victory just over two years ago, in June 1975. Dotted among the flag and pictures were what looked like scars of the liberation war in the form of fissures, cracks and holes – as yet unplastered and unpainted – the sort that could be caused by bullets and shrapnel. Had the armed struggle actually reached this far down south from the north of Mozambique, I wondered. I had until now believed that the actual armed fighting to free Mozambique from the yoke of its Portuguese colonialist rulers had happened in its northern rural provinces of Tete, Cabo Delgado and Niassa.

'There was some fighting here too,' explained the passport official when I asked. 'Support for FRELIMO in Maputo and other urban areas mounted following the movement's occupation of the areas it had liberated in the north. The enemy was met with return fire in the south as they went on a desperate rampage to destroy as much infrastructure as they could before they fled.'

I was filled with a sense of awe at witnessing at first hand and so soon this evidence of the birth of a new state from the barrel of a gun – and with a new exhilaration for finally getting here! Adding to the challenge of things to come was the stark contrast of these surroundings to the glossy sophistication of the airports in Lisbon and London, just fourteen hours away by air. I couldn't help noticing small things like the stuttering luggage carousel moving at a pace that suggested it might give up at any moment, and the battered luggage trolleys on wheels that mostly wouldn't turn.

'According to Beirao's secretary, who's just checked his diary, he was only expecting you next Tuesday. He's at a conference out of town till the weekend,' my immigration friend explained when I returned. 'The problem is he does not seem to have left your immigration clearance at the office before he left. Without it we unfortunately cannot allow you to leave the airport.'

I was devastated.

'You can use this office tonight while the university authorities make a plan to get you out,' he responded sympathetically but firmly when I suggested that I would leave my passport and other valuables with him for later collection if he let me out while my clearance was being resolved.

He offered me another cup of coffee to cheer me up, and also the opportunity to have a shower. But something told me that he was becoming over-friendly, so I declined.

'Go to the upstairs restaurant and have lunch,' he insisted. 'Here are some escudos if all you have is foreign currency.'

Again I declined.

'Please contact the ANC office in Maputo,' I asked him politely, giving him the telephone number. 'Tell them I'm stuck here and need to be cleared.'

He came back half an hour later to say he'd left a message at the office with the secretary of the ANC representative.

Two hours or so dragged by, during which I read several old copies of the newspaper *Noticias* and a few old magazines that the helpful official brought me. Eventually, at around half past three that afternoon, a wiry young man arrived at the immigration desk and asked to see me. He seemed well known by immigration, chatting casually with them for a while. Then, welcoming me warmly, he introduced himself as Comrade Jacob Zuma, from the ANC office in Maputo. Without hesitation he put my bags on the trolley and tried to push it towards the exit as I bade farewell to the immigration guy who had been so attentive. Little did I imagine he would trace my whereabouts and come to look me up.

On our way to the car, Zuma explained that, on receiving my message from his secretary, he'd had to phone the ANC's London office to check whether they had issued my security clearance for Maputo. Once confirmed, he came straight to immigration to clear and collect me. I had no idea, and of course neither did he, that he would one day be the deputy president of a free and democratic South Africa.

We reached his home at about 5 p.m. that afternoon. It was in a location of low-cost houses, neatly maintained matchboxes with tiny, well-kept front gardens. Zuma's wife Kate welcomed me with a cup of tea, then showed me the room I would be using. I showered, had dinner with the family and crashed.

At breakfast early the next morning, a Wednesday, Zuma was already busy phoning the university to tell them that he had rescued me from being held at the airport. Was there anyone from the Maths Faculty who was available to welcome me to the department? I also asked Zuma to check on my room at the teachers' residence. The previous night Kate had said that I could stay with them for as long as it took to clear up the confusion with the university. I was really grateful for this spontaneous welcome from comrades who clearly felt some sort of responsibility towards me, although we had never heard of each other before, let alone met. Just the fact that I was a comrade was enough for them. My first night in Maputo couldn't have been more reassuring.

The warmth of the Mozambican sun was a bonus after the long cold months in London. As Zuma gave me a quick guided tour of the city that morning on our way to the university residence – just around the corner from the ANC office, where he worked – I was struck by the stunning hotels, mansions and other buildings set against exotic-looking palm trees lining the coastal road next to the deep-blue Indian Ocean. This was in sharp contrast to the dilapidated shacks and *pondokkies* of the arid townships not far from the city. Déjà vu. I might as well have been in South Africa again!

The queues of people already waiting outside the shops were a sight that would soon become familiar because of the shortages of some basic foodstuffs and other consumer goods. This was caused by South Africa's decreasing trade with Mozambique, aimed at undermining its attempts to follow a socialist path of transformation and economic growth after its collapse through years of war – and because of FRELIMO's solidarity with the ANC.

'Welcome, Professora! Your room is ready!' the concierge, Senhora Alvez, greeted me at the door of the university residence as Zuma sped off.

Following coffee and an orientation chat, I unpacked. Then I took a walk to the ANC office around the corner, where I met the charming Lennox (his codename or *nom de guerre*), the chief representative of the ANC in Maputo – in effect our 'ambassador'.

That evening, Albie Sachs, the only other South African teacher still staying at the residence and a comrade I knew from London, took me for a walk around the local beaches and coffee shops. By my second day in Maputo I already felt at home.

The Christmas break from lectures had just begun. I had timed my arrival so that I would have enough time to find my bearings, improve my language skills, and meet and get to know some of my university and ANC colleagues before the rigorous teaching schedule started in January.

* * * * *

'Climb out of the window or we'll be stuck here all day,' ordered Rudi Westhuizen, an electrical engineer from Holland and a colleague at the university. I was sitting in the passenger seat of his car, staring in disbelief at the flood of water that had risen so high in the last couple of hours of heavy December rains that we could neither continue our journey nor open the doors to get out.

I took off my shoes, turned up my jeans, rolled down the window and sat on its frame. Then I slid out of the car, feet first, into the water. Rudi did the same. We waded through the waist-high water to the entrance of the nearby residence. The door to the ground floor was open, which was a small tiled area with nothing but a staircase leading up to the visitors' lounge and living quarters. The ground floor was flooded up to the fifth step of the staircase.

'Holy cow!' Rudi exclaimed as we approached Senhora Alvez at her desk on the first floor. 'Does this happen every time it rains?'

'When the rains are this heavy, yes,' she said. 'You see, as it became clear to the Portuguese rulers that FRELIMO was winning the war of liberation and that they would either have to accept a new government or leave Mozambique, they became really bitter. So before they started leaving, they destroyed as much infrastructure as they could, including the drainage system, using concrete to fill up the drains in many suburbs. So now the transport system collapses every time it rains heavily. Sewers, telephone lines, plumbing, electrical grids, air-conditioning, trucks for transporting agricultural goods from the rural areas into the cities – you name it, they messed with all of that to try and bring the place to a standstill.'

A stunning-looking, middle-aged so-called *mestido* (person of 'mixed blood'), Senhora Alvez became more and more agitated and angry as she explained the situation to us. 'But with the support of comrades like you, we will get the better of them, you wait and see!' she vowed.

It was a couple of days later, when the streets had dried up and we could start moving around again, that Professor Beirao organised a get-together at his flat. He had come to the residence a few days earlier to meet me and apologise for the confusion on my arrival. Now he had invited all Maths Faculty members who were still in town to a party so that I could meet them. Russians, Cubans, Italians, East Germans, Portuguese, Mozambicans, Belgians, English and Dutch *co-operantes* all came along. I was the only South African staff member in the Maths Faculty.

In his short speech to welcome and introduce me to my colleagues, Beirao referred to the floods we had just experienced as a small challenge in the bigger scheme of things that we, his staff, must embrace as a team, just like the engineers, chemists, physicists, doctors, agriculturalists, writers, linguists and other professionals who had come to work in Mozambique to replace the absconded Portuguese were starting to do.

Beirao told us that it was the blockage in ordinary Mozambican people's minds, created by the Portuguese rulers, and not the blockage in the drains of Maputo – which was easy enough to remedy – that was the real threat to the social and economic development of this newly liberated country. He said that it was our duty as mathematicians to contribute towards unblocking the minds of the many Mozambicans who believed, because of their previous inferior education, that university-level maths was inherently beyond their reach.

We would have to work together to redress this colonialist legacy by finding ways and means, including bridging courses, to attract and retain in our faculty as many secondary school graduates as possible. Such work would be in addition to one's current teaching programme and schedule.

'You, Zarina, will be teaching algebra and calculus to first and third years, and computer science to second-year students, as discussed in our correspondence,' he confirmed.

It was clear that the new bridging maths courses, which we would have to design from scratch, would not only have to ease high-school graduates – even those who had failed school maths – into university mathematics, but they would have to be taught in a fun enough way to attract and then keep them there.

I could not contain my excitement at this pioneering challenge that was being put to us, because, if successful, it would make a definite difference immediately by boosting the number of students enrolling for maths, and later in other ways. So, exciting as crossing new scientific frontiers at the Palo Alto Research Laboratories in California would have been, it would not have given me this sense – which Beirao was evoking so sharply as he continued to speak – of being at the frontiers of social change.

And what fun it would be too, working with colleagues from such diverse backgrounds and yet with so much in common, both politically and professionally. And fun we had! We were openly amused at each other's terrible and sometimes unfathomable Portuguese accents and lack of vocabulary, both of which improved with time, as we had no choice but to continue communicating in Portuguese, the only language we all had in common.

The advantage we had over members of other faculties was that, since mathematical laws are universal and the equations and formulae that express them transcend cultures and languages, we could simply write them on the blackboard to get our message across when words and grammar failed us!

The debates about a completely new syllabus were invigorating, so much so that they would often continue even during our time off, at the coffee shop, the beach, in between singing sessions with the Chilean and Cuban *co-operante* music groups, or at the swimming pool. How could concepts of pure mathematics for use in the workplace be reinforced unless they were applied through example? And, if so, would it be necessary to teach applied maths as a separate subject? In which areas of work critical to the immediate development needs of Mozambique would a firm grasp of maths be needed most? In terms of these areas, which branches of maths should we be prioritising? Should we use the modern set-theoretical or more traditional approach?

(Similar questions were also raised around a new maths syllabus for the recently established ANC school in Mazimbu, Tanzania, the Solomon Mahlangu School, where I was invited for a weekend to discuss these matters with educationists from the ANC in June 1978.)

Ruth First, a colleague in charge of the university's Centre for African Studies – and chairperson of the ANC's Education Committee – phoned to inform me one Friday afternoon in late February 1978 that the rector, Professor Ganhao, had called for a meeting with the committee in his office the following Monday morning. I was to be there at 8 a.m.

Made up of the four South African teachers at the university – Albie Sachs and Alfeus Mangezi were the other two – the committee had been set up earlier by the ANC office in Maputo. Ganhao and others were greatly concerned about a group of young people who had left South Africa after the 1976 Soweto Uprising, and who had been sent by the ANC in Tanzania – from the Solomon Mahlangu School in Mazimbu, where they had started studying – to the university in Maputo.

At the meeting the rector expressed his and his department's main concerns. Many of the students were in need of extra tutoring, some even at school level, he explained. There was also a lack of discipline in their ranks, which was causing increasing friction with their teachers and with some of their Mozambican peers. Could we help ease this problem?

Political classes for both the ANC students and staff, organised by the ANC office and a subcommittee of the Education Committee, had already begun, so these classes became a platform to address some of the concerns of the university authorities. It also fell to the Education Committee to provide the required extra tutoring.

Of the sixteen or so ANC students in Maputo at the time, five came to me regularly for extra lessons throughout 1978. Gradually I was able to build a relationship with them, and eventually they would drop by just to visit and listen to music, and chat about their families and about their dreams, which included returning home one day. I would encourage them, as my mother Jo had once encouraged me, to keep an even keel and try to become as skilled as possible.

Sadly, four of the five I tutored on a regular basis died young and mysteriously of illness in the eighties and nineties. A few of the others in the group, whom I did not know as well, also died like this. But before they passed away, most of those in the group had gone on to further their studies in Cuba, the German Democratic Republic (the GDR) and the Soviet Union, to become doctors, architects and engineers.

* * * * *

'The Ministry of State in the Presidency has made an urgent request for you to be temporarily seconded to the Presidency,' Beirao announced one morning in April 1978, waving a letter at me as I arrived for work. 'The Presidency wants you to do a feasibility study on computerising the government's information system.'

The system was then held in bulky files that were falling apart, and their processing had become too time-consuming and inefficient.

'When do they want me to start?'

'Next Monday,' he replied.

The work was piling on! So I took advantage of that weekend's voluntary manual work scheme for *co-operantes* to get away, this time to clean out the machines and premises of a cashew nut factory near Macaneta. I was keen because I knew my Cuban colleagues had volunteered for that weekend, and they always made manual work sessions loads of fun with their guitars, singing, dancing and the jokes we shared during our breaks.

'There were some people looking for you this afternoon,' Senhora Alvez told me on my return on Sunday evening. 'I told them you'd be back around now.'

Just as she finished the sentence, the doorbell rang.

'If it's for me, please say I've been delayed,' I said. 'I'm really too tired to see anyone right now.'

She obliged. I peeked over my balcony, which overlooked the

Jo with Aunt Sarah
and Uncle Dieter

Ami and Jo on their
wedding day in 1935

With my first love, Jeffrey,
in Troyeville, 1945

Jo with her
sister Naomi, 1956

Jo with Ami (centre) at a bridge awards ceremony, 1954

Performing with Mayibuye in the seventies. From left to right: Ronnie Kasrils, me, John Matshikiza, Billy Nannan, Melody Mthetwa and Barry Feinberg

With friends in London, 1973. Dulcie September, far left, later the ANC Chief Representative in France, was murdered in Paris by SA security apparatus in 1988

London march with activists after the murder of comrades in South Africa, 1976

With Mac in Mozambique
in the late seventies

Our wedding day,
27 February 1981

Our unconventional
marriage officer

Lebo, Karabo, Bernard,
me, Carl (a colleague),
and Mac in Maputo

The family, just before Mac went underground, 1988

Mac and Milou

Milou's 6th birthday, five days after Mac left on the Vula mission

From a magazine article, emphasising our lives in exile. (I'm suppose to look like a mother hen with my children under my wing!)

With Father Trevor Huddlestone
outside South Africa House, London,
agitating for Mac's release

Campaigning in Holland for Mac's release

Handcuffed and manacled to a policeman,
Mac attends his sister's funeral in Brixton, Johannesburg

ice escort ... detained SACP and ANC member Mac Maharaj, surrounded by policemen and manacled to one of them attended his sister's cremation service in Brixton, Johannesb
yesterday. He was not allowed to talk to anyone, including his lawyer   ● Picture by Stephen Davimes

Nanda, Beverley and me hiking near Corfe Castle, Dorset, 1991

Joey turns seven, Yeoville, 1991

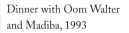

Dinner with Oom Walter and Madiba, 1993

Mac, Joey and Milou on Table Mountain, December 1997

The family with
Stevie Wonder and
his then partner,
circa 1997

At the opening
of the road near
Qunu in the
Eastern Cape.
The road had been
built entirely by
women during
Mac's tenure as
Minister of
Transport

Photo: Jürgen Schadeberg

Having fun with
Graça and Madiba
on Mac's birthday,
1998

With Graça Machel
at Mac's birthday
luncheon, 1998

With Oom Walter
after a lunch
in Observatory

The family
with Madiba

front door, to see who my guests were, and recognised Indres Naidoo. He was with Bobby Pillay (real name Sonny Singh) and Mac Maharaj, who was based in Lusaka. Indres and Sonny, two other recent ex-Robben Islanders who had just settled in Maputo as full-time functionaries of the ANC, were leading the way back in the direction of the ANC office around the corner.

I was disappointed to have missed this chance to see them, and also relieved that it was not the passport official, Paulo Kapesi, pestering me again. He had come to the residence soon after my arrival to look me up. On the first occasion Albie had let him in. We had coffee, chatted, then subsequently met quite often. But I got fed up with him when, for the third time, he asked me for some foreign currency. I refused yet again. Although I told him not to visit me any more, he continued to come over and ring the bell insistently, even after Senhora Alvez refused to let him into the residence. Eventually he took the hint. I realised then how much I would miss her protection when I had to move out to my own flat!

Mac joined me for dinner three days after I started my term of secondment at the Presidency. It was 23 April 1978. I was very excited, and a bit nervous too, at being alone in the company of someone who was a legend in South Africa's liberation struggle. What if he found me boring?

But at the same time I was also very wary of Mac, as I had learnt that he was a communist, and my experiences with many of the communists I'd met had been unpleasant. I thought I would therefore not see eye to eye with him.

There was also the question of his marriage to Tim. Rumours were doing the rounds that they had separated, but I wasn't sure of this. I therefore felt completely restrained in his company, despite my attraction to him – and, as I knew by then, his to me.

As the weeks passed, we would meet whenever he was in Maputo on ANC work. These meetings gradually helped calm my apprehensions about getting emotionally involved with him. I found Mac very balanced in his opinions, forthright about the reasons for the break-up of his marriage and honest about what he wanted out of life.

Eventually I began to relax, and allowed myself the full pleasure of his company.

* * * * *

Towards the end of June, a week after handing in my feasibility report to the information chief at the Presidency, it was announced that in early July the Maths Faculty would be relocating from downtown Maputo to the more distant new campus on the coastline towards Costa do Sol. I had to make a plan for transport, as I would no longer be able to rely on my rickety bicycle to get me to lectures every day. A car was out of the question, as I was repatriating over a quarter of my modest salary to London to pay off my half of the debts in England. So, one Friday afternoon I took a bus across the Namaacha border to Manzini in Swaziland to buy a motorbike, even though I'd never ridden one before in my life.

That Saturday morning I bought the last 120cc motorbike available in Manzini, a gorgeous blue Suzuki. That evening, while I practised riding the bike on quiet roads, a traffic cop stopped me.

'Where is your crash helmet? It's an offence not to be wearing one,' he barked at me angrily. He had followed me for a while, then waved at me to pull over as I approached a set of traffic lights in the city centre.

'And the registration plate for this bike? What about your licence to ride this?' he bombarded me.

I didn't have anything. So he made me get off the bike – which he stressed I was not legally entitled to ride – and push it two kilometres up a steep hill to the police station as he followed me slowly in his van. At the police station, I told the policemen that I was just a teacher in Mozambique needing transport. They did not seem to believe me once they realised I was South African. Eventually, after two hours of interrogation, they allowed me to go to my hotel to fetch my passport and other documents to verify my story.

At the time, the Swazi government, tempted by offers of financial assistance if they played ball with South Africa, had already begun to turn on those of its neighbours who were sympathetic to the ANC. Having entered into a collaboration arrangement with Pretoria – for which they were being richly rewarded – they had also started turning on the ANC in Swaziland. Luckily they didn't know that I was an ANC member.

The police did not lock me up. They let me return to my hotel, but held onto my passport. The shop owner who'd sold me the bike that morning, and who had inadvertently set me up by offering to supervise my riding lessons that same evening, was waiting for me. He had disappeared into thin air when the police apprehended me.

Mac, who'd quietly been hard at work in Manzini all day, was also there. I was furious with the shop owner, and told him so. Fortunately, the next morning he took most of the blame for my transgression of Swaziland's traffic laws. He sorted out the matter with the police, who let me off. As compensation, I suppose, he gave me an oversized crash helmet (the last one in the shop). Comrade John Nkadimeng, who was working with Mac, was not impressed.

'This loose helmet certainly won't protect you if you have an accident. Put your bike on the next train to Maputo,' he implored. 'It will take about a week to get there, but that will be safer. There are just too many dirt tracks, and steep hills and valleys on the road to the Mozambican border.'

He was genuinely worried. But I had made up my mind. 'This challenging trip will give me a good feel for the bike and make me an experienced rider,' I tried to reassure Comrade John. 'It is mostly on highways, and once I make it there, using it in Maputo will be a piece of pie.'

The owners of the shop where I had bought the machine escorted me in two of their bakkies to the outskirts of Manzini, where they watched me get the hang of the machine. They were very worried that I was taking too much of a risk trying to ride back alone to Maputo when I had never before even been on the pillion of a motorbike. Perhaps they felt guilty for having inadvertently set me up for trouble with the cops!

As I was waved off that Sunday morning in late June by my anxious escorts watching my faltering start back to Maputo, I couldn't help but whoop out loud with elation at the sense of self-reliance and freedom these two wheels had already given me.

*　　*　　*　　*　　*

'*Desculpe-me! Desculpe-me, camaradas!* [Sorry, sorry comrades!] Please don't shoot me. I did not see the barrier!' I screamed in panic at the guards a few metres ahead when I realised that I had gone through an almost invisible piece of metal wire strung across the road, a makeshift barrier, and that they were now training their AK47s on me. Even with the front headlamp on, it was too dark for me to see the flimsy barricade on the stretch of road between Maputo and the Namaacha border.

'Why were you going so fast?' asked the fat guard. 'Show us your passport and your licence!'

I handed over my international car driver's licence, written in English – which the guards could neither read nor speak – and passport. Of course, the licence did not entitle me to ride a motorbike, so I was shaking in my boots. While the one studied the documents, the other asked me where I'd been, what work I did and so on. Then he too examined my licence. I couldn't thank them enough when they told me I could continue my journey!

I was even more jubilant at the sight of the beautiful wide boulevards, lined with imposing palm trees and lit by quaint street lamps, as I approached Maputo via nearby Matola, where I had on two occasions gone with Mac to a 'transit' house for cadres on their way to South Africa. There I had waited with some comrades in the garden while he had meetings with others in the sitting room.

Little did I suspect then, or even now as I rode past their street, that fifteen cadres of Umkhonto we Sizwe would later be massacred in a surprise attack by invading soldiers of the South African Defence Force – in flagrant contravention of Mozambique's territorial sovereignty. 'A challenge to the very concept of African statehood,' President Tambo was to protest bitterly at a memorial service for the victims of the massacre.

It was past midnight when I leant my bike against the stairwell in the entrance foyer of the residence. Senhora Alvez had advised me to do that when I returned. Mac heard me arrive.

'What took you so long?' he asked, clearly relieved that I had made the journey in one piece.

We had left Manzini around the same time, he in a car belonging to the ANC. Yet I arrived eight hours after him! But rejuvenated by being together again, we celebrated my safe return with a toast. While I had a shower, Mac unloaded the bike – of my personal belongings, and the brooms, biltong and Dr Scholl shoes Pam dos Santos, wife of then Vice-President Marcelino dos Santos, had asked me to bring her. That's when Mac noticed that the bike's headlamp, instead of pointing forward, was facing down onto the front wheel.

This had probably happened when I fell and the bike went flying at the first petrol station as I was leaving Manzini at 11 a.m. that morning. I had accelerated when I meant to brake as I approached the petrol pumps. Or it could've happened when I skidded on the deserted dirt road where, luckily, I revved away in time from a truckload of Afrikaans men who hissed and made lewd remarks when I refused their offer of a lift. They'd wanted to load my bike onto the back of their truck.

'No wonder you had to travel so slowly in the dark and took so long to get here!' Mac laughed.

'Never mind,' I said. 'I've made it, and what I want more than anything now is to unwind, relax and let my hair down.'

We set off on the motorbike for the beach at two o'clock that Monday morning, returning to the residence only at 5.30 a.m., in time to get ready for work.

Whizzing along the coastline to campus for my 7.30 a.m. lecture that morning, with the sun already warm and the ocean breeze streaming through my hair, I was ecstatic with life, thrilled with the exciting challenges of my work, with the new freedom to make my own choices and decisions, and with the new love I had found. The sight ahead of someone anxiously thumbing a lift, something I had often had to do myself in the recent past, brought me back to earth. Screeching to a halt, I realised it was Gebuza.

He got onto the back seat, and though his destination involved a bit of a diversion from my route, I was more than happy to take him there, as I had often seen him walk in the debilitating heat past the residence, sweating profusely, sometimes stopping to ask for water, then pressing ahead on foot to do his work. At the time there were few cars available to the ANC, and public transport in Maputo was in a state of collapse. Gebuza and I were to cross paths again in Zambia through an ANC project we both got involved in.

So giving people lifts became an everyday thing. Battered single-decker buses, often appearing unroadworthy, were mostly so crowded with passengers – the influx of people from the rural areas was already putting a strain on urban services – that many would be jammed onto their entrance and exit steps, clinging for dear life to any railings and handles within reach to stop them from falling off. Even the rear fenders would often have passengers standing squashed against the back of the bus, precariously holding on to the window frames.

In comparison, a ride on the backseat of my bike was something of a luxury, especially when the sea breeze cooled the humid heat of the Mozambican sun. Even Joe Modise, who would later become democratic South Africa's first Minister of Defence, managed to squeeze his huge backside onto the backseat of my bike!

Within months, other *co-operantes* – including another female teacher at the university – started going to Swaziland to buy themselves motorbikes too. Then we occasionally raced each other at night along the coastline, a bit like Hell's Angels. But riding a motorbike was not without its problems. Truck drivers mainly could be quite disdainful.

Then there was the time in November that I took Simone Chimowitz home after having lunch at my place. She was a young teacher from Zambia working at the English-medium International School in Maputo, attended mainly by the children of *co-operantes*, diplomats and other foreign workers. We suddenly smelt something burning, like food on a stove. But neither of us could spot any hawkers on the pavements roasting mealies or other foods.

As the smell grew more pungent, I stopped to check if perhaps my tyres were burning from the scalding hot tar road. That's when I noticed a light vapour coming from Simmy's left leg, which was resting against my blisteringly hot exhaust pipe. The bit between her ankle and calf was burning! With her nerve endings damaged by advanced diabetes, she felt nothing. In shock, we turned around and headed towards the hospital to have her burns attended to.

CHAPTER 8

A place of our own

Seven months into my contract, in July 1978, and I was still on the waiting list for a flat. Albie had three months earlier moved out of res on the same day that Graça Machel, the beautiful young Minister of Education – she was just thirty-two at the time – and wife of the president, came to the university in the morning to address the teachers. Praising us for our work, she then asked us if we would please dress more appropriately.

'Your blue jeans and sandals are not right for the classroom,' she started. 'It is not in line with our ethos and philosophy. Nor does it befit you, ladies, to come to teach in such informal tank tops,' she continued gently.

'As for your long hair,' she looked at a few of us, 'please either tie it up or cut it short. Our revolutionary values require this.'

That afternoon, in spite of having to move out to his own place, Albie took time to go to the barber to get an atrocious-looking short-back-and-sides – it took me some time to get used to his new look after his long curls – while I went to buy comfortable court shoes and elastic bands to make a ponytail. Years later, when I reminded her of that speech, Mrs Machel burst into loud laughter. 'Our goals at the time demanded it,' she said.

Now I was the only South African left at the residence. On occasional weekends I would get away with Mac to Ponto d'Ouro – from where we once crossed illegally onto a Natal beach on foot – or some other hideaway. On other weekend afternoons I would walk the streets of Maputo checking for empty flats and houses that looked available for occupation and that I could tell Senhor Xavier about. He was the administrative official – overworked and a bureaucrat if ever there was one – responsible for allocating university housing.

Senhor Xavier had warned me earlier that I would have to wait quite a while for a place to move into, as the government had nationalised housing in 1975 and Mozambicans and expatriates alike, in private and public sector employment, were queuing to be accommodated. The rents were now so low that workers who previously could not afford to live in the abandoned homes of those who had fled had now started occupying them. So I was delighted when he came to the faculty to offer me the keys to a flat on the sixth floor of a block on Avenida Tómas Nduda.

'It's terribly run-down. Check if you want it and let me know,' he said.

'If you have an hour, let's rush there right now,' suggested Sonny Singh, who was having coffee with me at the time.

He was a member of the Internal Political and Reconstruction Department, of which Mac was the secretary, based in Maputo. The team lived and worked at the 'White House', which Frene Ginwala's family had donated to the ANC. Sonny had sometimes accompanied me on my searches for a place of my own.

Now that I had the flat keys, he felt as happy for me as I did. But I was worried about Sonny rushing around, because the Mozambican heat could play havoc with his health. Sonny had a metal plate in his head. An irate co-prisoner had crushed his skull with a spade for no apparent reason in the lime quarry on Robben Island. On one of our earlier searches for an empty place, he had suddenly thrown his spectacles to the ground in a rage and stamped them to a pulp, cursing loudly all the while. It turned out that the metal plate in his head had become so hot from the sun that the extreme pain drove him crazy.

In spite of his suffering, even while still on the island, he had refused, on principle, to lay a charge of assault against the comrade who had battered him so cruelly. The more the prison authorities egged him on to lay a charge, the more Sonny refused, such was his sense of solidarity with his comrades and his contempt for the enemy. I felt privileged to have him as a friend.

'Don't forget your hat,' I urged him as we set off to see the place on Avenida Tómas Nduda.

It was in a terrible state, the filthy carpet moth-eaten, with large burn marks in places. The dilapidation and dinginess was even worse in the kitchen, where the previous occupants seemed to have done the cooking on a brazier in a corner of the tiled marble floor rather than on the stove, with the walls around that area covered in greasy stains. There was also some damage to the walls in the bathroom and two bedrooms.

But here at last was the complete privacy Mac and I had become so impatient for, tucked away far from the madding crowd.

Although Xavier had the place cleaned out and the walls repaired, I would have to furnish it myself. But by now there were growing shortages of affordable household furniture and fabrics. Like food, there was less and less on the shops' shelves and in their windows.

PW Botha's government was trying to force FRELIMO to stop ANC cadres from using its borders to cross into South Africa by curbing trade with Mozambique. This situation worsened the already ailing Mozambican economy, caused by the exodus of most of its professional, technical and skilled business and labour force.

South Africa also drastically cut the number of Mozambican migrant workers to its mines, badly affecting this source of foreign currency earnings in Mozambique and creating serious unemployment in the country. Yet with all the hardship suffered by ordinary Mozambicans, they and their government continued to show a strong sense of solidarity with the South African struggle.

A young Chilean group took the gap in the furniture market. They started producing cheap but stylish basic tables and chairs, using the bountiful local wood still available. For the rest, after lectures I started going to the sawmills located among gigantic trees on the outskirts of Maputo, where I would buy my own wood.

'Please cut me a piece from that tree. Here are the sizes.'

What an awesome sight to watch tree trunks three to four metres in diameter, still rooted in the ground, being sliced with automatic machines to whatever size I wanted. There were trunks of lesser diameter, but to make my life easier I wanted to make desktops and table tops that would have no joins at all. These pieces, still wet with sap and smelling green, would be delivered to the flat by truck, where they would be dried out flat on my large verandah for at least a week.

The smaller pieces I would carry back from the sawmills on my motorbike. While these were drying out, I would seek advice and borrow tools from colleagues and friends accomplished in DIY, some of whom occasionally popped in to help me. Never before or since had I experienced setting up home like this, with furniture fresh from the soil, so to speak, at a fraction of the cost I've ever paid! For curtains I used cheap dress material that I had lined to make it look more substantial, a trick my mother had taught me.

So impressed were Zuma and Lennox that they brought ANC cadres, who were living in the sparsely furnished ANC hostel-type dwellings in Matola and other ANC residences, to the flat to show them what could be done despite the shortages. Even Xavier started bringing home some *co-operantes*, even though he had opposed a structural alteration to the flat that I had proposed we make at the outset. Knowing he was actually keen to improve the government's homes, where possible, and that he would like and approve the alteration once he saw it, I had risked defying him. The risk paid off.

'Trust a South African to do this!' Nascimento Mhlongo, a Mozambican colleague and neighbour, exclaimed when he entered the flat. 'What happened to the wall?'

I had had a non-supporting wall smashed out the first weekend I moved in, the one Xavier had said I should not remove. The resulting light, space and airiness had enhanced the place a lot, Nascimento agreed. So had the wooden floors, sanded down and restored to their original beauty once I had ripped up the carpets.

*   *   *   *   *

Many people living in the peri-urban and rural areas – especially where there were no roads – had no physical addresses, and their dwellings could therefore not be recorded in any government register. Fieldworkers were employed by the Housing Ministry to go out and identify such homes and allocate physical addresses to each one.

It was now early August 1978, and the fieldworkers were returning to Maputo with their lists of residents and the addresses they had been allocated. The Maths Faculty, having recently acquired a brand new Bulgarian-manufactured mini-computer, was asked by the Housing Ministry to assist in creating a database of this new information. Ferraz, a Portuguese Mozambican who was heading the project, roped me in because of my recent work for the Ministry of State in the Presidency.

At the Presidency, following my report on the feasibility of computerising its information system, I had written to the major Western computer manufacturers – including IBM in the USA and ICL in the UK– for quotations for machines that would meet our system requirements. I did not receive a reply. When I pressed for a response from them in follow-up letters, they said quite frankly that they would not sell their computers to a country in which they would be 'risking' their physical presence to back up and support their machines.

This response was consistent with the tacit support of their governments under Reagan and Thatcher – through their 'constructive engagement' with South Africa – for PW Botha's policy of 'destabilising' Mozambique, with its socialist agenda and its support for the ANC, through military and economic pressure. In the end we got a Bulgarian computer manufacturer to supply the Presidency.

Now the Maths Faculty had also been supplied with a computer by the same Bulgarian company.

This extra workload meant I had to stay on campus till late some evenings. Fortunately Vanda de Angelis, with whom I shared an office, was also very busy at the time, so she too would have to stay late. We would go to the canteen together, have coffee and talk lots.

A thirtysomething Italian statistician from the University of Rome, with impressive accolades for her work both at home and recently in other parts of Mozambique, Vanda and I found we shared a love of music, fashion, the movies and maths. Like me, she was separated from her husband, and had found a new man. Our friendship blossomed and I learnt a lot from her.

At this point I also started learning from Ruth First, especially about the art of relaxation. On occasional Sunday mornings I would join her on the ferry across to Katembe, where we would swim in the sea, have a late lunch and go for a walk, then return to Maputo to take in a movie. It was instructive to note how she could switch off so totally from work on these occasions, one of the secrets, she told me, of her immense productivity,

As the director of the Centre for African Studies at the university, she guided, among other research projects, a study on the impact of migrant labour to the gold mines of South Africa on the Mozambican economy. When the South Africans reduced this stream of revenue to the Mozambicans, Ruth had the means of quantifying its economic effects.

Her book *Black Gold* was about South Africa's gold mining industry in general, and its use of black migrant labour from South Africa's 'bantustans' and the southern African region in particular. Other research projects the centre was involved in under her direction included looking into ways of breaking South Africa's economic stranglehold on the region, as a means of opposing that country's plans to bring the region to its knees.

A Marxist committed to Mozambique's then socialist path to transformation, Ruth loathed Stalinism, which she admitted openly, eliciting the wrath and derision of those in the London exile circle who defended it. In my discussions with her, I realised that she did not take this personally: rather that the atmosphere in London's exile community was closed and claustrophobic, demanding that one conform in order to be accepted. One could see the sheer relief in her of having got away from there, how she revelled and was growing in the atmosphere of independent Mozambique.

As a result of my friendship with Ruth, I came to accept that my problems in London had not been about me as a person.

Ruth's intellect and commitment cost her her life. In August 1982 she was assassinated by a letter bomb sent to her by the security forces of South Africa. Pallo Jordan, later a cabinet minister in democratic South Africa, to whom I had introduced her in 1978 when he visited me during his first trip to Maputo – he memorably helped clean my flat during that visit – was at the scene of her gruesome death. The sound of that bomb blast affected his hearing in one ear.

Vanda was a Marxist of Ruth's ilk. Like Ruth, she listened to other viewpoints, never simply dismissing questions that were provocative. Always ready to engage in fair, congenial debate, she often drew on interesting examples from history to substantiate her views or refute mine. In this she shared with Ruth and Mac a more humane, open-minded side to being a communist.

Though I still did not subscribe to a Marxist paradigm of society and the world, Vanda and I got on like a house on fire. My experience of the intolerance of so many of the communists I had met earlier had actually led me to believe that I could never be friends with one! Yet even before he resigned from the South African Communist Party in 1989, Mac and I had become true friends.

I introduced Vanda to Mac. As he got to know her better, he saw her potential to help the underground at home. As an Italian committed to our struggle who was totally unknown to the South African security forces, she was an ideal person to smuggle weapons into the country. By the next vacation, this was what she was doing. The weapons were concealed by cadres in Mac's team specially trained in the task – in the insides of her car doors, in the roof, under the floor of the boot and wherever else concealed compartments could be made. Vanda always performed her tasks willingly, sometimes accompanied by her nine-year-old son Daniel, who had no idea what his mother was involved in. On one occasion she was met in South Africa by Amin Kajee, 'Doha', with whom Mac had worked closely in the underground in the early sixties.

Vanda's quiet courage and modesty were a breath of fresh air after the cloying 'I'm a Red, so I'm better than you' attitude of the communists I had associated with before, who were in truth as green as grass when it came to assessing the real march of history, as the collapse of the Soviet Union in 1990 proved. How could the 'only' horse in the race lose the race?

Now that my flat was ready, it was time for a housewarming party. But there was a problem. Would there be enough for my guests to eat? The food shortage was getting worse. Mozambicans had been allocated monthly food coupons for their basic rations of oil, mealiemeal, bread, sugar and so on, while expatriate *co-operantes* could use their foreign currency allowance to go to Swaziland – a collaborator state with South Africa, which had everything anyone could need – to stock up on supplies. Many *co-operantes* went there, especially from the diplomatic corps. But this was an expensive option compared to scouring the fish and vegetable markets on a regular basis for unexpected deliveries from local fishermen and nearby farms.

Luckily for me, when I could no longer stomach the rice and *carapáo*, a small, bony, dried fish tinier than any sardine, which we ate every day for months on end at the 'Self' (the self-service canteen for university staff and students), Mac arrived one day from Swaziland with enough supplies to last me a few weeks, including luxuries such as bread, cheese and dried fruit. He had illegally crossed the Swaziland border into Mozambique on foot in the dead of night, carrying a large rucksack of arms on his back, with my supplies in it.

Mac and others had often moonlighted illegally in this way, but this was the first time he carried groceries too. Rudi, my Dutch friend, felt a little upstaged by this, as his kitchen had become something of an oasis for some of us. Not only had he brought a freezer from Holland, which he would fill once a month with fresh supplies from Swaziland, his pantry shelves were a treasure chest of tinned foods and biscuits, which he would bring in from his working trips to Europe.

*   *   *   *   *

'It's a deal, Raoul!' I exclaimed when my neighbour Nascimento's youngest brother, a fisherman at weekends and a student during the week, offered to sell me some of his Saturday morning catch so I could have my party. The only provision was that I invite him and introduce him to Therésa, one of my second-year students, whose parents had just moved into our block.

'You must be there as the boats begin to come in, at 9 a.m., before Raoul's regular customers arrive,' Nascimento advised. 'Be ready by 8 a.m. I'll take you there.'

'First, wood straight out of the soil, and now fish straight out of the sea! And look at those palms and that sky! No wonder they call this the Jewel of Africa,' I enthused as we walked along the beach towards the car that Saturday morning, carrying the fish from Raoul's boat.

'We'll be a hard act to follow once this country is on its feet,' Nascimento responded proudly. 'It will take years, but we'll get there, watch!'

The party was in full swing when Raoul came over to me.

'There's an unshaven, long-haired hippie type at the door asking if you live here. Should I let him in?'

I went to check. It was Mac! I'd last seen him six or seven weeks ago, just after I'd moved in. He'd suddenly gone off somewhere on work, and had clearly been too busy to cut his hair.

'I didn't recognise this place. What's going on here tonight?' he asked.

Not expecting him, I was thrilled by this surprise visit, my excitement soaring at holding him close again. From this moment we would grasp every opportunity to bask in the joy of having found each other after years in our respective emotional deserts.

'I'll join the party after I've taken a bath,' he said. 'I haven't had one for weeks!'

The flat was milling with university colleagues, students, and ANC comrades and friends. As we got into the groove and the fun grew – I had not expected Ruth would so love to dance to the sound of Motown! – we could not have imagined that fourteen of the people at this party would die violent or untimely deaths. As was the case with struggle activists, many were known by a *nom de guerre*, and others only by their first names. And, losing touch over time, we never got to know the real names of some.

'Ralph' and 'Jessica', a young ANC couple revered by all who knew them, were visiting Maputo on work from Tanzania, mingling happily with everyone at the party. 'Obadi' was present too, staying at Matola while preparing at the time for his team's devastatingly successful attack on Sasol's oil refinery, something I was only to learn about him later.

'Ashwin' was there, one of Obadi's team who would go on the Sasol mission, as were Gebuza and his brother 'Douglas'. And so were 'Blackman', Ruth, Paul Dikeledi and his Mozambican wife, the Mozambican journalist Carlos Cardoso, and Bernard, Phumla, Zama and Dineo, four of our students from the 1976 Soweto Uprising.

Chillingly, Ralph and Jessica turned out to be highly trained informers working for the South African regime. Ralph was implicated in the murder of Douglas and some of his team in Swaziland in the mid-eighties, at the hands of Eugene de Kock from the notorious Vlakplaas, a base near Johannesburg for the apartheid state's killing apparatus. De Kock had led the attack on the house where Douglas and his group, including Ralph himself, were staying. Of course Ralph managed to escape during that attack.

Years and many other deaths later, in the early nineties, Ralph and Jessica were detained by the ANC. They apparently admitted to being agents of the apartheid regime. Ralph died in detention. When the ANC was once again legitimised in South Africa, Jessica was one of those released from detention.

Obadi – his real name Motso Mokgabudi – was one of the fifteen MK guerrillas to be killed in the January 1981 Matola raid by the South African Defence Force as a result of informers passing on information to the South Africans about his daring attacks on the strategic Sasol oil refinery. Ashwin – or Krishna Rabilal rather – was also murdered in the Matola Raid. South Africans who had been tipped off about his movements killed Paul Dikeledi in an ambush in Swaziland in 1984. Blackman was poisoned, also in Swaziland, which, by 1978, had been fully co-opted by South Africa to work against the ANC.

Bernard, Phumla, Zama and Dineo – among the vibrant young students who had helped me choose the music and cook the food for the party – died of an undisclosed illness, two of them as early as 1980. AIDS was their suspected killer. Ruth was killed by a letter bomb, sent by South African security forces to her office at the university in August 1982, just three weeks after visiting me and my newborn son, Amilcar, at the home of Beverley and Nanda Naidoo in Watford, near London. And in 2000 Carlos Cardoso was killed by some of his Mozambican countrymen, whom he'd been working to expose for extortion and fraud.

As early as June 1978, just before I went to buy my motorbike, Mac had left me for a night with some dynamic young men and women in a 'safe' house on the Swaziland side of the Namaacha border while he went off to do some work. Within weeks of that occasion, the house was razed to the ground when South African agents planted bombs against the outside walls, killing all the people I'd just met. Welcome to the war of liberation.

* * * * *

In the short academic winter break of June 1979, Mac took me to Lesotho to meet his mother. They had last seen each other in early 1977, just before his sudden escape from house arrest at his younger brother Kithar's flat in Chatsworth, Durban, following his release from Robben Island in late 1976. Like Mac's father, who died while his son was in prison, his mother Lily had missed Mac terribly during his twelve years on Robben Island. She had wanted to see more of him on his release from prison, even though she applauded his escape from house arrest when she learnt of it.

Now, being driven by Kithar and his lovely wife Mayna to Lesotho, Lily was thrilled to be meeting her son again. This was the first time she had ever travelled outside South Africa.

Once Kithar had crossed the Lesotho border, he phoned Mac from a public phone box to a safe phone they had earlier arranged. As South African security was deep in the throes of its 'total onslaught' on the ANC and its allies, we could not be careful enough. The brothers arranged a secret place in Maseru where we would all meet in a few hours' time.

At the venue, a comrade, Bob Machi, hosted a welcome party for Mac's mother. To my delight and wonder, small and slight, white-haired and clad in a matching white sari, she took over the party completely, becoming its life and soul! Clearly deeply excited to hold, touch and be with Mac again, she told us many stories, in her broken English, of his escapades over the years. Mac often interjected, ragging her about some of the things she herself had said and done in loathing of the system that had taken her son so far away from her. She even told a strapping blond Russian engineer who attended the party that, over the years, she too had become a communist!

'You're a white communist, I'm a black one,' she teased, to roars of laughter. She also encouraged Father Lapsley, a New Zealand priest in Lesotho sympathetic to the ANC who had lost an arm opening a South African letter bomb, to keep up his courage fighting apartheid. When Mac gibed that she never gave him the same sort of encouragement, Lily replied there would have been no point, as he did his own thing anyway. Their rapport as mother and son soon became evident and was heartwarming to watch.

Before we'd left for Lesotho, Mac had asked me to take extra money along, as his mother was extremely concerned about how he would continue to survive as an unpaid political activist, and he wanted to reassure her that she had no reason to worry. We agreed to splash out on her to put her mind at ease, especially as there was no telling when we'd see her again.

On the Saturday morning after Bob Machi's party, we took Lily to Maseru's main shopping centre and told her she could choose whatever she wanted to take back to South Africa. We paid the money so discreetly that Lily thought she was being spoilt by the shopkeepers, who recognised Mac from his newspaper pictures following his escape from house arrest and were sympathetic to his cause!

But the biggest laugh I got from her that weekend – and there were many – was when the five of us were out eating at a restaurant. Lily had never been to a restaurant before. Mac urged me to put Mayna, known to be a secret smoker by her mother-in-law, at ease, by accepting a cigarette from him. Though not a smoker myself, I did so. Lily, feigning disapproval, turned to her sons.

'My sons, you both like pretty, pretty women, but like pretty apples, cut through, what you get? Full worms!' she said in her broken English.

Yet this episode seemed to relax her because, having earlier refused a glass of wine – again something she'd never experienced – Mac was now able to coax her into tasting a tablespoonful. She loved it and asked for another! Even the sight of mixed couples entering the restaurant was something completely new to her.

'Does this sort of thing happen here?' she asked, astonished.

We connected so well that she insisted on putting food in my mouth at lunch the next day, in effect her way of showing her acceptance of me. So when Mac was contacted, in 1983, and told that she had died four months earlier of a perforated ulcer – apparently he couldn't be reached earlier – I was as devastated as he was. That was the first time I saw Mac cry. He had so wanted to see more of her, wanting her to come and join us outside South Africa.

So much had Mac loved Lily and so strongly did he feel about the right of women to inherit, that when he was in prison with not a cent to his name nor any prospect of a paid job on his release, he refused to accept his share of his late father's property, insisting that his mother take what was left to him instead. Traditionally, the women in his family did not inherit anything.

That first image of tiny Lily in Lesotho in her lily-white sari with her lily-white hair, with her enormous warmth and infectious sense of humour, remains as vivid as ever.

*   *   *   *   *

I was growing more nervous as the sun disappeared, dusk fell and still no motorist had passed me by. About thirty kilometres north of Maputo, I was stranded alone on the roadside at a deserted beach on this weekday in mid-November 1978, wearing nothing but a wet bikini, with not even a towel to shield me from the chilly wind.

I had ridden straight to Marracuene, near Macaneta, after lectures at 3 p.m. that day, to get away from the city to this place of solitude I had come to love, a place of peace and quiet where I could take stock of things and try to clear my mind.

I had swum a couple of kilometres into the calm, warm ocean under the clear sky, lost in my thoughts and in communion with nature, when my motorbike keys, clothes and towel were stolen. As always, I'd parked the bike on the beach and left these items, as well as my books, in its locker on the pillion. But this time I'd hung the key to the locker around my neck, thinking – mistakenly – that I'd locked it.

The front wheel of the bike was locked into a forty-five-degree angle to its frame, so, dripping wet when I reached it, I struggled to pull it up through the sand to the road to look for help. There was not a single person in sight. But suddenly a white Land Rover appeared, travelling quite fast, with its headlamps on bright. It screeched to a halt when I waved it down.

'Get in, we'll go to my place,' the driver suggested in English, probably thinking I was a prostitute who picked up foreigners! His Afrikaans accent told me he was South African, and his clothing that he might be a naval officer.

I pointed to my bike, and in Portuguese explained that my clothes and keys had been stolen, and that I had to get the bike to Maputo. I pretended I was Mozambican, and even made up a name when he introduced himself as 'Piet' and asked me what my name was, as I did not want him to know I was South African. I was afraid of anyone in Mozambique who even looked like part of the South African military.

On our way to Maputo, between large swigs from a bottle of whisky, which he tried to make me drink too, he told me that he was part of a 'maritime force' guarding Mozambique's fishing waters against illegal poachers – but I still suspected he was there to monitor the ANC's activities!

When he became more insistent on going to his place, because his 'sheets were clean', I said mine were clean too. He became extremely excited, and did not try to hide his readiness for action. I directed him to Albie's nearby block of flats. Standing at the entrance was Sonny Singh. Spotting me half-naked with what looked like 'the enemy', he seemed momentarily bewildered, and turned away as if he hadn't seen me. I shouted at him to get me a towel. While Sonny fetched the towel, I told Piet that he should help Sonny unload the bike when he came back. When Sonny returned, I wrapped myself in the towel on the pavement and managed to let him know what was up, then quickly disappeared into the building.

Sonny told Piet he'd fetch some more men to help unload the bike, and went to Albie's flat to call two comrades as backup. The three of them sent panting Piet packing once they'd retrieved the bike. That's how I got out of that one! Sonny's face, his mixed expression of shock, disappointment and confusion when he spotted me wearing almost nothing in such unlikely company – could I be two-timing his friend Mac? – still makes me laugh.

Some years later, in 1988, the South Africans made an attempt to take out Albie. A popular member of the Law Faculty at Eduardo Mondlane, he was later to become a judge in South Africa's post-apartheid Constitutional Court. Blown up by a bomb planted in his parked car outside his block of flats, he miraculously survived, but lost an arm and the sight in one eye. Clearly even ANC teachers at the university had become fair game for South Africa's killing machine.

A month or so after the Piet saga I started returning to the beach near Marracuene on occasion, now more aware of the dangers, though. On one such excursion, around September 1979, my heart was pounding faster than usual as I swam swiftly towards the horizon, my thoughts tripping over each other in a mixture of excitement and confusion. The night before Mac had asked me to marry him and live with him in Zambia!

He stressed that he had nothing in the way of material support to offer me, that his ANC allowance of 14 kwachas ($5) per month was unlikely to be increased in the foreseeable future, that it could buy him just a monthly tube of toothpaste, a couple of toilet rolls and a bar of soap, and that his allocated weekly supply of one kilogram of meat, two kilograms of vegetables, some rice, oil, tea, dried milk and sugar was sometimes supplemented with the odd tin of food, like tuna or beef, from the Soviet Union. Then there was *mpande*, the annual allocation to cadres of some new shoes and clothing.

I already knew all of this full well, and it didn't matter to me one bit, hopelessly in love as I was with him. What did bother me, though, was how our relationship would be affected in the longer term by his status as a struggle 'aristocrat' and a hero of the South African people, compared with my 'commoner' status as an ordinary member of the ANC.

I feared that if I became Mac's wife, the disparity in political standing between us would compromise my separate identity, especially as I was considering working for the ANC full time after my Mozambican university contract expired. Would I be able to cope with such an assault on my independence and individuality if I married him? Would I be able to live without him if I didn't? I was damned if I married him and damned if I didn't!

But love has its own logic. So I followed my heart. Rather than renew my Mozambican contract when it expired, I would join Mac in Zambia. As it turned out, we would not have been able to see that much more of each other had I stayed on in Mozambique after 1980. The economic collapse and political fragility effected by the South African government to force FRELIMO to police the presence of ANC cadres in the country and reduce their numbers had already borne bitter fruit: the terrible suffering of ordinary Mozambicans from ever-worsening shortages and rapidly growing unemployment.

Reluctantly, FRELIMO would have to bow to the economic

pressure and military raids from South Africa in return for peace and economic support. Even before 1980, Mac and others started being detained at the airport for not having the 'right' documents. I once 'rescued' him from the airport, and before long there was a massive security hunt on for us. But I returned him after dinner, before they caught up with us. Despite their hardships, the strong underlying sense of solidarity Mozambicans felt for our struggle never waned.

I was not in Mozambique during the worst three years, which led to the signing of the Nkomati Accord with South Africa in early 1984. The Accord officially denied the ANC access to South Africa from Mozambican territory, and led to ANC activists in that country being relocated to Zambia, itself suffering similar economic and military pressure from South Africa.

Little did I suspect, as I was packing up to go to Zambia, that the challenge of trying to retain my identity, and not being perceived as just 'Mac's wife', would eventually be overshadowed by the intrigues and onslaughts that lay ahead for us.

PART IV

Going into Battle

CHAPTER 9

Boldness, be my friend!

LUSAKA

It was a cold winter's night in Roma Township, towards the outskirts of Lusaka in Zambia. Mac and I were living in the maid's quarters some 300 metres behind the big main house on a very large property. As I pointed the cocked Makarov pistol towards the thick, dry, waisthigh grass, my finger resting on the trigger, I trembled, and not from the icy wind! Suddenly, like a bolt out of nowhere, a huge figure lurched up and ran away at breakneck speed into the pitch dark towards the back fence. I had been told to pull the trigger if I ever believed we were in danger. Instead, I stood, transfixed, as this apparition disappeared into the dark night.

I immediately returned to the main house to inform the comrades in Mac's team – the ANC's Internal Political and Reconstruction Department reporting to the Revolutionary Council – of what had just happened, and within seconds one of them was searching the spot where someone had been hiding. While he was looking for clues as to who it might have been, another two comrades guarded us with their AK47s.

'Look at this!' shouted Garth Strachan, one of the comrades from the main house. He picked up and waved a small stool on which the intruder, hidden in the tall grass, had sat. The stool had been positioned in a spot some ten metres away from and directly opposite the front door of the maid's quarters, conveniently blocked from view from the main house, not only by the tall grass in which it was hidden, but also by the smaller building's solid back wall, broken only by the high, tiny slit of the toilet window.

For some time that evening I had had the eerie feeling that we were being watched, and now my uneasiness had been justified.

Mac had left for Swaziland that afternoon, and I didn't feel like being on my own as darkness fell, as I'd had something of a premonition that morning that trouble might be lurking. It being a Saturday night, I decided to join the comrades in the main house for supper, cards and Scrabble. One comrade, who should have been on duty that night, had to be away, so I was asked to help with his guard duty. On the hour, every hour, one of us would walk around the yard checking that everything was in order before the all-night guard for that weekend was to take over at around midnight.

Before it was my turn again to go outside and inspect the property, an inexplicable feeling, that someone was right in the yard, suddenly overwhelmed me. I decided not to wait my turn this time. Instead, not wanting to seem paranoid – I had been getting increasingly restless and fidgety, and was clearly working on the comrades' nerves – I made an excuse to go and fetch my eye drops from the back cottage. I took my pistol from the sideboard, cocking it on my way out. But I did not take the usual route on the well-lit path that went around the right side of the cottage to its front door.

Instead I headed towards the darkness of the thick, bushy patches to the left of the building. I was so nervous as I made my way out of those dark bushes and towards the brightly lit front door, that I was pointing the pistol in front of me in readiness for an attack. Emerging like this from the dark, in full view of the intruder, my pistol at the ready, he must have assumed we had spotted him and had come to ambush him. But before I could even register that someone was there, he was up and away, like a phantom in the dark.

'Look at this!' Garth yelled again, picking up a half-smoked packet of Gauloises cigarettes, a torch and a copy of the *Daily Telegraph*, which had been lying by the stool. It looked like the man could be a foreigner, perhaps British. But the scarier part was still to come.

We soon discovered that all the handles on the windows of the maid's quarters had been removed, making it impossible to lock them. We deduced that the intruder knew that Mac and I lived in this house, and that he'd been lying in wait for us that night. If he could not finish us off outside, he was planning to get in through the windows to do so.

'Sleep in the main house tonight,' Mandla instructed me. Mandla was also known as Peter, and it was he who had trained me in the use of the Makarov and the AK47.

'You have no choice,' little Dawood – a young musician who had been taught by Abdullah Ibrahim, a doyen of South African jazz – insisted.

But there was a large filing cabinet, which contained files that related to the work the comrades were doing, in the kitchen of the maid's quarters. So they decided it would be better if Mandla and Garth stayed with me for the night.

We were busy barricading ourselves in with boxes and furniture, and securing the windows with wire hangers, when we heard a strange noise outside. Mandla radioed the main house to switch off the mains so that all the outside lights would go out, then he and Garth unbarricaded the front door. They insisted on locking me in, and, with the advantage of knowing the large yard better than any intruders could, stealthily checked it with their AK47s loaded and cocked, ready to shoot in the direction of any noise.

Then a cat, which I spotted through the window, its eyes glistening green in the pitch dark, knocked over a bottle in the open shed nearby. This was exactly the noise we had heard earlier. It was not, after all, the prowler who'd returned! Still, I'd now seen at first hand just how brave and battle-ready these young comrades could be in the face of a threat, and it left a deep impression on me.

*   *   *   *   *

Although it was not remotely as beautiful and cosmopolitan as Maputo, I was delighted to be in Lusaka. We might as well have been living in heaven, so happy were Mac and I to have moved in together.

We painted the place, and when my goods arrived from Mozambique, put in a rug or two, posters, plants, a lamp and a tiny table, which I made from off-cuts of a shelf that had got charred from the heat of the exhaust pipe on the truck that had brought it to Zambia. The place soon felt so homely, we had the Angolan and Indian ambassadors and a few comrades over for a housewarming party.

It was in this period that Comrade Nkobi (or 'TG'), then treasurer general of the ANC, explained to me that, where possible, one spouse should be earning an independent income to relieve the organisation of the escalating costs of providing accommodation, transport, petrol, food and so on to the families of activists, as such support was increasingly diverting much-needed funds from the underground political and military structures operating within and around South Africa.

'We owe it to the Zambian government to save them the thousands in foreign currency that it has to pay to the British each year for the work they want you to do,' TG advised me. 'You can and must do it.'

As it happened, the detailed terms of reference of my job at the University of Zambia were still being settled between the Universities of Cambridge and Zambia. I had been offered the job of 'Zambianising' Cambridge University's computer-based system in order to process the nationwide final-year, pre-university Zambian school examinations, but had not yet signed the contract.

Though I had previously been very keen on being deployed in the ANC, now that I was with Mac I was in two minds about this, especially as I didn't want anyone in the movement thinking that I was piggybacking on his struggle reputation. Cherishing my independence, I felt relieved at the guidance and encouragement TG had just given me. Then I signed my contract. Now I was once again on a university waiting list for a flat.

*   *   *   *   *

'Tell Hans that's an AK47 in your gym bag,' I urged Mac as we started unpacking our few items of luggage in Hans and Gerda Büttner's guestroom. They had kindly agreed to put us up for the night. 'And tell them why we're here. It's only fair.'

It was the early eighties. The apartheid regime's 'total onslaught' on those of its neighbouring states that were harbouring the ANC was intensifying, and included military raids by its Defence Force into these states. ANC Security and Intelligence would alert the ANC membership if such a raid seemed imminent, and we would have to move out of our homes to try to secure our safety. On this particular evening we had been warned to find safe homes. We hurriedly packed two small bags after we had phoned Hans and he had agreed that we could sleep over for a couple of nights. But Mac did not tell him why we had to stay with them.

Gerda and Hans had welcomed us with their usual warmth. As we were making our way down the corridor towards the guest wing, I noticed the shock in Hans's eyes when the bath towel covering the AK47 rifle, which was hidden in one of the bags, slipped off and he saw the barrel. Hans said nothing, but was clearly alarmed.

So, over a pre-dinner drink, Mac explained to Hans and Gerda why we needed a place to stay, adding that we were actually putting their family at risk with our presence.

'Now that we have told you the truth, you must tell us the truth,' Mac said. 'Tell us if you prefer that we don't stay here tonight. We do have other options of safe houses. It's just a matter of a phone call.'

Hans gulped down his whisky.

'Would they even suspect you were here?' he asked.

'They shouldn't know, but it's not impossible that they might find out. So, please guys, be honest with us,' Mac urged.

Shaken, Gerda asked Hans to join her in the kitchen, where they talked for a good ten minutes or so. When they came back to the living room, Gerda announced that if they couldn't risk their safety for ours, they couldn't claim to be our friends.

'You are welcome in our home, especially at times like this,' she said warmly.

I was so touched by this spirit of solidarity, I couldn't hold back my tears. Gerda, a talented German artist in her mid-thirties, had often told me that those Germans who had done nothing to protect the Jews from Hitler's genocide were in some way responsible for their deaths. She seemed to carry huge guilt about that part of being German. Now it was as if she felt she had an opportunity to atone in some way for Hitler and the Nazis' deeds.

'And what about Vera and Olaf's safety, and Hans's job with the Friedrich Ebert Foundation if your home were to become a target?' I asked. Vera, nine, and Olaf, three, were the apples of their eyes.

'We've made up our minds,' she said, and hugged me warmly.

So began a deep friendship between our families. The Büttners even tried to visit me in Sussex in 1990 during the time Mac was in jail, while the 'talks-about-talks' for a peaceful South African settlement were proceeding. But Joey was ill in a paediatric hospital in Brighton and I had to postpone. Hans was by now a member of the German parliament in Bonn, working with a group of parliamentarians specialising in African affairs.

Gerda had become a local government councillor in Ingolstadt and a popular artist in Germany. Some people had a tendency to describe her as 'apolitical'. But, a freethinker and free spirit, she always put her money where her mouth was – in more ways than one – when it mattered. Was her act of making her home a safe refuge for us when we needed it a 'political' one? Does it matter what we label it?

When Gerda and Hans returned to Germany in 1982, we found other safe houses as the military raids into Zambia continued. Later on, when the children were still in nappies, we would have to pack up their feeding bottles and all their other baby paraphernalia – once even their cots! – and move out fast. When they were at nursery and primary school, their clothes, school uniforms, school bags, books – the whole toot – had to go with us. In all the chaos of such sudden moves we often misplaced and lost a lot of things, including, at times, my confidence that we would see freedom in our lifetime!

Sadly, our dear friend Hans died suddenly of a heart attack in 2004, after visiting us in democratic South Africa three times, once with Gerda.

During this period in Lusaka I would often have to stay at the university very late in order to ensure that the localisation targets were being reached, including the hands-on training of the Zambian team. About ten months into my work, in February 1981, a technical team arrived from Cambridge to assess our progress for themselves, and whether the British government, through its Overseas Development Administration (ODA), should adopt the proposal of the Zambian government to start paying my salary as part of a technical aid package.

The Cambridge team arrived on Friday 27 February 1981, the day Mac and I had booked to get married at the local council offices, or Boma. I had to go to work that morning, as the team was to return to Cambridge shortly, on the coming Tuesday. I would excuse myself by midday, as I didn't want to lose our deposit again to get married. On a previous occasion, Mac had missed the appointment because he was held up in Swaziland. Though he too went to his regular Friday Revolutionary Council meeting that morning, this time he made it to the Boma.

'Would you still marry him if he had only one eye?' the official marrying us asked me on that scorchingly hot afternoon.

Barely able to contain my giggles, which had started earlier in the ceremony, I burst out laughing at this question. The official was not amused at all.

'I've already warned you that if you continue to disrespect this ceremony, I will not marry you,' he said, irate. 'I mean it. So pull yourself together now.'

I bit my lip, took a deep breath and avoided eye contact to try to control myself. Thankfully Mac looked away too, so I was able to keep a straight face for the moment.

'Would you still marry him if he had only one eye?' he repeated.

'Yes,' I answered meekly.

I dared not tell him that in fact Mac did have only one eye, for fear of losing my composure again and delaying the ceremony even more. (As a student at Natal University, Mac was stabbed in his left eye in a fight, and was fitted with a glass eye.) As it was, the ceremony had got off to a late start. The official had pitched up only at 2.35 p.m., when our appointment had been for 2 p.m. By then my bouquet of flowers had already started wilting in the heat of the afternoon, and my mascara had started to run. So I put on my sunglasses for the ceremony.

'How can you come to be married dressed like that?' the official had snapped as we walked into the registry office. Mac was wearing a flecked maroon shirt with an open Indian collar and black corduroy trousers – he had rushed to the Boma from his meeting – and I was wearing my favourite dress, a frilly black Biba frock.

'This is a sign of disrespect, not only for this important ceremony, but also for the president of the Republic of Zambia,' the official said, and gestured to a picture of President Kaunda on the wall. 'I'm not sure that I should be marrying you.'

'What about the dirty line inside your collar and the holes in your socks?' I thought, amused but poker-faced. 'Chill, man, life goes on.'

'You freedom fighters,' he had started off the ceremony, addressing

Mac. 'I know you people. You marry women wherever you happen to be stationed. How long do you intend to stay married to this woman?'

Mac grinned. 'Forever, I hope.'

'Stop your grinning and answer this question. Do you really love her?'

Mac looked serious this time. 'Yes.'

'Is this the line of questioning in all civil marriages in Zambia?' I wondered, really starting to enjoy myself after quite a heavy morning at the office. I had believed this would be like any other civil wedding ceremony I had attended, with marriage vows, signatures, and over in twenty to thirty minutes. But this was turning out to be a blast!

'And would you still marry her if she had only one eye?' he proceeded to ask Mac, almost aggressively.

'For sure,' Mac replied, straight-faced. We couldn't risk his wrath any more by appearing less than serious.

Once satisfied that I would marry Mac even if he too had only one eye, he asked me:

'And what if he had one arm?'

'Yes, sir.'

'And if he had one leg?'

'That would be difficult, but I would, sir.'

What next of Mac's anatomy, I panicked. Is he heading for his manhood? Would I have to say 'yes' again? Luckily he spared me that question.

I stole a glance at our witnesses to the marriage, Ray Alexander and Gerda Büttner, seated along the wall behind us, and their spouses Jack Simons and Hans. Ray once memorably told me that the labour pains while giving birth to a baby are nothing compared with the pain of giving birth to a book. She was referring to her experience when she'd co-authored the classic *Class and Colour in South Africa* with Jack. Now the tears of laughter streaming down her face set me off again. I burst out laughing uncontrollably.

'This is my last warning to you. I'm calling off this marriage unless you show the necessary decorum,' the marriage officer reprimanded me again.

Decorum? His line of questioning had hardly showed decorum! Fortunately the phone rang at that moment and he answered it, giving me a chance to get a grip once more. Luckily Mr Decorum changed tack at this point. From his earlier tirades about unfaithful freedom fighters and disrespect for the Zambian president, he began something of a eulogy.

'You people fighting such a noble cause, so far from home and family, have to marry, sadly, without owning even a suit or tie. Not even a suitable dress. For this South Africa will honour you one day. I truly wish you everything of the best in your life together. Now put the ring on her finger.'

'I don't have one,' Mac answered timidly.

It was Mr D's turn to assume Mac was joking.

'No, seriously,' Mac repeated. 'I don't have one.'

'And you don't mind?' He looked at me incredulously.

Quite honestly, I didn't, because we'd had no time to shop around for a ring. I didn't have one either. I told him so.

'Pretend you have one, then, and make as if you are slipping it onto her finger,' he suggested somewhat sympathetically.

We went through the routine, Mac slipping a make-believe ring on my finger, then I on his, while Jack and Hans's cameras flashed away, capturing the moment.

'Now it's time to sign the marriage register,' he continued.

At which point Gerda and Ray got up to sign as our witnesses.

'Wait till I tell you to do so,' he reprimanded them, adjusting his grubby collar so that he would look the perfect marriage officer in the pictures he wanted taken of us signing the register under his watchful eye. Only when he was in the right pose did he allow the cameras to start flashing.

By now over an hour had passed and even the flower in my hair had begun to wilt. All I wanted was to go and celebrate. But in the register we had both filled in 'Divorced' under 'Marital Status'.

'Please may I have your divorce certificates?' the official asked politely.

'Oh, my goodness. We didn't bring them!' I exclaimed.

'Just as you didn't bring the ring, the suit and a nice dress!' he flared.

Now he had the perfect reason to cancel the marriage as he had kept threatening to do.

'You are not actually legally married,' he informed us.

Then, yo-yoing in mood again, he offered to let us off.

'You may regard yourselves as married while you find your divorce certificates. You have two weeks to get them here. Otherwise the marriage is off.'

Then he shook our hands warmly and wished us the best for the future.

We felt lucky to have made it! No one witnessing the marriage had ever experienced anything like it before. But at least we had laughed all the way to the altar. Now there would be an even more festive atmosphere at the wedding dinner Ray and Jack were hosting at their home that evening.

The next day Mac had to leave for Botswana and I had to continue discussions with my Cambridge colleagues. I met them at my office at the university's Computer Centre. Fortunately there was no chance of a repeat performance of what had greeted me on a couple of occasions when I'd first arrived: live chickens, owned by a staff member who sold them on the side, flapping their wings and squawking loudly as they frantically flew through the well-equipped computer room with its sophisticated mainframe and peripherals, while staff members ducked and dived out of their way!

Though an exception to the normally ordered environment of the computer room, this sight – bizarre and hilarious though I found it at the time – might have raised doubts in the Cambridge team about the wisdom of the technology transfer we were working on. As it happened, following our meetings that weekend, I was later appointed 'TCO', or technical cooperation officer, by the ODA, its highest ranking in technical aid. I had no idea at the time how Mac's detractors would use this position to get at him.

*   *   *   *   *

It was early evening, about 6 p.m. in mid-May 1982. A car was driving extremely close to us as we were walking back from the Chimowitzes' home in Kabulonga to our place nearby. I could actually feel it pull up. For a moment I thought it might be a friend offering us a lift, as I was by now very heavily pregnant with our first child. But instead four armed men jumped out, their faces covered in stockings and scarves.

They ordered Henning Hintze, a German friend, to the other side of the car. 'You, stay here,' they told Mac and me, who were standing on the grass verge that acted as a pavement.

I heard them demand Henning's wallet and watched over the bonnet as he gave it to them. But Mac refused to cooperate. One of the men kicked him in the stomach, while the other one, in a red scarf, punched him in the face. When he fell to the ground, the red-scarfed man pulled out a gun and aimed it at him.

Without even thinking, I threw myself on top of Mac, pleading that they shoot me instead. The gunman hesitated, clearly taken aback at this unexpected turn of events. In that moment I could feel Mac's right hand trying surreptitiously to reach under my huge stomach towards the holster on his left. But before he could reach his Makarov, they dragged me up, and ordered him up too. They took Mac's pistol, got into the car and sped off.

In the few seconds that Mac was lying on the ground, he had memorised the number plate on the car. His mouth and nose bleeding, we started searching for his glasses, which had landed in the gutter.

'I would have shot those bastards if I could have reached my gun without them noticing!' Mac said.

He was very agitated. But Henning and I were relieved that he couldn't get hold of his Makarov. If he had tried to shoot any of them in our defence, all three of us could have been killed. Shaken, we returned to the Chims, who helped calm us down. Then Mac phoned ANC Security to tell them what had happened. A comrade called Keith arrived with a couple of others, armed with semi-automatic rifles and a pistol or two. They gave Mac a weapon and they all left to deal with the thugs. There had been a robbing and killing spree in the area for a few days now. They felt it was time to do something about it.

But the men just couldn't find the car that night, and returned a couple of hours later, determined to track down the criminals in the morning.

The next day we learnt that, within twenty minutes of the attack on us, a French couple, also out walking, were seen being accosted by four thugs, one with a red scarf, who had pulled up alongside them. But this unlucky couple were not just robbed – they were killed. What had made them spare us? Someone suggested that my pregnant stomach had unnerved them. Another thought they would somehow have realised that we were members of a liberation movement with the capacity to hunt them down, with or without the help of the police. At any rate, we felt lucky to be alive.

*   *   *   *   *

Nineteen months into my contract with the university and with just two-and-a-half months to go to the baby's delivery date in July 1982, I was in the throes of finalising my second annual progress report for Cambridge and of selecting someone I could start training to act as systems manager, to oversee the project during my maternity leave. Mac and I were both still so ecstatic about the baby's forthcoming arrival, we had to restrain each other from shouting it from the rooftops!

After tossing around some names, including Dedan, after the 1950s Mau-Mau leader in Kenya, Dedan Kimathi, we settled on Amilcar if it was a boy – after two other heroes, Amílcar Cabral, the African leader of the struggle for independence in Guinea Bissau from Portuguese colonialism; and Hamilcar Barca, the general from Carthage (in ancient North Africa) who was the first African ever to defeat the invading Romans. He was also the father of Hannibal, who famously crossed the Alps. (When some of our French friends in London first saw Amilcar, at only two days old, they immediately nicknamed him 'Milou', a play on the second syllable of his name.) And for a girl, I loved the Sotho name Dineo, meaning 'gift'.

I had been very busy at work for almost two years and relished every moment of the challenges that came my way. Although I often missed Mac terribly during his frequent absences, I was able to put this time to good use and go the extra few miles in the hands-on training and skills development programmes we were designing and implementing to bring our Zambian staff up to speed. They would soon have to take full responsibility for the running, maintenance and upgrading of the system.

It was during the course of this work and following Amilcar's birth that I was invited to attend some ad hoc meetings of the ANC committee looking into computerising various administrative and information systems in the organisation.

'I told you you'd do it!' Comrade Thomas Nkobi, the ANC's treasurer general, enthused on the phone to me one morning in early 1984. 'You make us very proud.'

He had watched the news on TV the previous evening covering our public launch of Zambia's own national school certificate system, where much was made of the large savings in scarce foreign currency this would mean for the Zambian government because, for the first time in its history, the country would be totally independent of Cambridge University's expertise in this aspect of its education. All the hard work had paid off. Our team had made it!

The 'Cambridge School Certificate' had given way to the 'Zambian School Certificate', a small advance in Zambia's ascendancy over its educational affairs, but one that was much celebrated by Zambia's educationists, memorably by then permanent secretary at the Ministry of Education, Mr Banda, who declared his intention to kidnap me from the university and keep me at the Ministry!

It was only after August 1984, when I'd had my second child, Sekai Jo – named after the gentle Shona midwife (Sekai means 'smile') from Zimbabwe who delivered her, and my late mother Jo – that the reality of juggling my roles as the sole breadwinner and a virtual single parent, intent on giving my best to both roles, hit me. Even with the help of some close friends and comrades, I found it a difficult balancing act. My attempts to keep an even keel just could not fill the growing void Mac's increasing absences from home were starting to leave.

In this period of apartheid's heightening repression and brutality, and its 'total onslaught' against its political opponents inside and outside South Africa, Mac's clandestine work in the front-line states was rapidly intensifying. By 1986 he had additionally to undergo almost a year of further training in military and other skills in various countries sympathetic to our cause, including the Soviet Union and the GDR, in preparation for his own secret entry into South Africa to carry out Operation Vula, OR's brainchild.

So, whenever Mac could be at home with us, he tried to squeeze a minute out of every second. He would try to do everything at once: play with the children, read and tell them stories, change their nappies, feed them, and, when they were older, take them to crèche or school, and even to some political meetings.

147

Once, when I had to be away, he tried to simulate breastfeeding my inconsolable baby daughter by stripping down to his waist, like I would do to feed her at night, coaxing her to suck from the bottle that he had stuck in his armpit. It worked. She obviously thought this was close enough to the real thing! I don't think my father ever bottle-fed any of us, or even saw, let alone smelt, a soiled nappy. My mother would have loved Mac for so many other reasons too.

So, when Mac had to leave town, Milou would routinely stand at the door around suppertime – even when he was as young as two – hoping his dad would somehow reappear and join us at the table. Joey, starting when she was still in her pram, would excitedly hail every passing white car on the road, believing it was Mac's. Often the children would not let me cut their nails or hair, insisting that their dad did it better.

It became a ritual to make greeting cards or pick flowers from the garden to welcome Mac home. Mac missed us a lot when he was away, time and again overcompensating for his absences on his return. Not surprisingly, Milou and Joey started seeing his erratic reappearances at home as visits from Father Christmas, wonderfully exciting but all too brief.

So, when Mac could be in Lusaka for a few weeks at a stretch, this was cause for celebration. One such occasion was over Christmas 1986. I bought a Christmas tree. Friends from Harare and Botswana would be joining us for a week. I had invited several comrades, including Joe Slovo, for Christmas lunch.

On Christmas Eve we were decorating the tree and starting to prepare the big lunch for the next day when OR arrived and asked Mac to fly off somewhere urgently. We were horribly disappointed, not least because this underscored the limbo of our lifestyle, the pointlessness of planning even small events.

But Milou and Joey put on a brave face once some sort of explanation was forthcoming. As they grew older and came across children who'd permanently lost their fathers, whether in the struggle or otherwise, I would remind them just how lucky we were to have Mac around at all. But I dare say this was like telling a hungry child that, because there were starving children in the world, they should not feel hungry. Or that it was selfish of them to want their father home more often because he was away trying to help make a better life for all South Africa's children.

Late in 1984, I made a final visit to Cambridge University, to discuss the proposal of Mr Banda of the Zambian Ministry of Education, who wanted Cambridge to support the renewal of my contract with the ODA. This would allow me to transfer the newly developed exam system from the university to the Ministry's new in-house computer facility and train some additional exam officials in its use. During this visit I learnt from a young MK cadre visiting London from a military training camp in Angola about the gossip that had been doing the rounds in Lusaka. According to the gossip, because Mac and I had been living in an upmarket residential area for diplomats since our marriage and Mac was wearing smart clothing, our improved lifestyle could only be attributed to a source of income above and beyond any salary I was earning at Zambia University. This income was generated by spying on the ANC for British MI5, under the guise of my working for the British ODA.

As unchecked rumours are wont to do, this one was gaining momentum and assuming a life of its own. But nobody ever actually confronted me, interrogated me or locked me up, unlike some other suspected spies. For example, Pallo Jordan, now Minister of Arts and Culture, was kept in an unventilated corrugated iron hut in the extreme summer heat of Lusaka for six weeks and fiercely grilled for allegedly fraternising with 'the enemy' in Angola. But then the intention of our detractors was to keep us smeared through hearsay.

Naturally Mac raised the issue in an appropriate structure of the movement. When his request for evidence of my 'spying' activities produced none, we expected such slanderous prattle to die the death it deserved. But a few gossipmongers in the corridors of power would not let it go. As it happens, such early attempts to vilify us were just a foretaste of things to come. I had no idea what we had done to deserve this.

I had become aware quite early on, while still living in the maid's quarters at Roma Township in 1980, that Mac's forbidding record in the struggle over the past twenty-five years – in the underground, in prison, in international anti-apartheid structures and in MK – together with his outspokenness, readiness to disagree on and debate issues with anyone in any forum, his uncompromising attitude to work and his sense of urgency about it, had resulted in his detractors in the movement labelling him an 'unapologetic' Indian, one who did not know his place in the struggle.

At the time, Mac, as secretary of the Internal Political and Reconstruction Department (IPRD), was specifically responsible for the political mobilisation and organising of the ANC underground inside South Africa.

As a member of an ethnic minority that had in apartheid South Africa been afforded more privileges than the African majority, he was regarded by some as neither contrite nor deferential, nor compliant enough about this: he was 'too big for his boots', in other words. 'Arrogant' became the word his detractors used to express this resentment towards him.

'The problem with Mac Maharaj,' the late John Motshabi, to whom Mac had reported in the IPRD, based at Roma Township, once said, in Mac's presence, 'is that when you close your eyes when speaking with him, you would think you are speaking with an African.'

Obviously some comrades thought Mac was mistaken to believe that being equally in the struggle, he was equal in the struggle. However, Mac also had many supporters in the movement. At the Kabwe Conference in 1985 – when, for the first time in the history of the ANC, non-Africans were voted into its leadership – Mac was elected to the National Executive Committee. It just never occurred to him that his ethnicity required, in the minds of those who were so offended by this 'upstart' Indian, that he be more restrained and less forthright in his views and interactions, that he take more of a back seat.

But that would have gone against everything Mac had fought for, everything he valued, the many precepts underscored on Robben Island, notably by Madiba, his friend and mentor, who had vowed, even under threat of a death sentence at the Rivonia Trial in 1964, to fight *any* form of racial domination.

Mac's attitude to these issues was not to think of himself in ethnic or racial terms, but that each of us should do the work we were given and do it properly. He forged ahead regardless, and unapologetically, and was later handpicked by OR himself to command Operation Vula inside South Africa.

As we were to learn later, this only riled his detractors more.

Fortunately for me, caught up as I was in these political under-currents as Mac's wife, I had so much work to do as a full-time working mother and the breadwinner of our family that I was completely focused on achieving the goals I had set myself, and could mostly ignore these intrigues. I had to conclude the renewal of the British ODA contract with the Zambian government, and train cadres – including Lebo, whom I'd tutored in Maputo – to use publishing software in part-time work I had been asked to do by Barbara Masekela in the ANC's Department of Arts and Culture, which she then headed. I also had to complete my preparation for prospective work with the United Nations, and spend as much time as possible with my beautiful young children, whose innocence was like a gift from heaven in this difficult milieu.

So enamoured was I with Milou and Jo, so keen on meeting my work targets, and working so hard to strike a harmonious chord between home and work, that these political undercurrents flowed like water off my back. But one day they were to become a raging torrent.

*   *   *   *   *

One night in 1987, when Mac was away, I heard the sound of intruders outside my house in Kabulonga, which had come as part of my ODA package. The dog's barking, which had woken me up, was growing more frenzied. Raids on ANC personnel in Zambia by the South African security apparatus had been mounting – we had occasionally to move out for a night or two with the children and all their paraphernalia.

I couldn't be sure who the people outside were, and, as there was no sign of the security guard, I took the AK47 from my wardrobe, loaded it, locked the door of the children's bedroom and, to scare off the intruders, opened fire from the bedroom window in their general direction. The commotion must have woken the security guard, who came running from the front gate at the entrance to the long driveway, asking what had happened.

It was only when the dog's barking had subsided that I responded to Joey's cries to let her out of the room she shared with her brother. But Milou wasn't with her. It was only years later that he was able to talk about this incident. He told me that the dog's barking had woken him up, and he went into the study. The curtains were open, and he saw some men, their faces covered in balaclavas, blowtorching their way through the burglar bars on the window.

Terrified, he came to alert me, but found me loading the rifle. Struck dumb by panic and unsure whether the men would break through the burglar bars, he went to hide in the lounge. Upon hearing the sound of gunfire, he assumed the worst, and he lay behind the sofa, frozen in fright, until we came to find him.

*   *   *   *   *

Later that same year, some months prior to my joining the United Nations after my spell at the Ministry, I met Tim Jenkin for the second time. I had first met him in Maputo nine years earlier, when he and Alex Moumbaris, a fellow prisoner at Pretoria Central Prison with whom he had been serving time for their underground work in the ANC, had escaped and made their way to Mozambique.

Tim was in Lusaka to discuss, with Mac, the possibility of setting up an underground computer-based communications system. He returned to Lusaka for follow-up meetings a couple of times in the next few months.

In early 1988, I was on a break between winding up the ODA job and starting the UN job for the Preferential Trade Area (PTA) in Lusaka. During this time I spent a couple of weeks with Tim in London, helping him test the prototype of the communications system on the public phones in the city. Testing at the exposed public phone boxes inside Selfridges on Oxford Street in London's bustling West End was quite nerve-wracking, as queues to use public phones in central London were quite long that fortnight. The crowded Christmas sales were on, and several people waiting in line got really fed up with me for taking so long.

The software Tim had so brilliantly developed could convert a typed message for transmission into a cryptically encoded one, an audible equivalent of which would then be generated and played into the mouthpiece of a public telephone and transmitted as a digital signal down the telephone line into a receiving computer with the same communications software.

This software would enable the encrypted signal to be decoded and converted into the original typed message and displayed on the receiving screen, all at the touch of a few buttons to select the required menu items. Potential users of this friendly system could be trained to use it quite quickly. In the case of a private telephone line, a modem would directly transmit the message digitally down the line without the need to play its audible version into a telephone mouthpiece.

Once Tim had ironed out the bugs we picked up during these tests, and I had moved from our secure ODA home to our new, equally secure UN home, we installed the communications software on my private desktop computer in the study, the first such installation in Lusaka. That was the original node through which Tim, in London, would safely relay messages from Mac, once he was inside South Africa, to OR and JS in Lusaka.

On the afternoon of 4 July 1988, Mac and Gebuza left Lusaka to enter South Africa illegally. As D-Day drew nearer, I began to face up to my fears for Mac's safety, which I had deliberately been shutting out of my mind until then. Now that the reality was sinking in that he might not come back home alive, and my denial was giving way to dread, I began to question for the first time whether, if he did not make it back, I would have the strength to shield my children from the shock and upheaval this would mean to our lives. Milou was five days away from turning six and Joey five weeks away from turning four.

On 3 July, on the eve of their departure from Lusaka, OR, Gebuza, Mac and I had dinner together. The children were in bed. Before and after dinner the men carted all kinds of packages and other items, which they had been storing in my study, to Gebuza's car. The determination in Gebuza's eyes that night reminded me of how he would doggedly persist in mastering every small detail of the communications system during our training sessions.

'I never want to get stuck using this system,' he'd explained his tenacity.

At the table, OR, a teetotaller, toasted the gathering with apple juice. He had earlier told Mac and Gebuza that the only failure of Operation Vula he would accept was if they returned to Lusaka under threat of capture or death. Later he spoke to Mac and me alone, acknowledging the painfulness of the path we were about to walk and assuring us both that he would look out for the children and me.

OR also expressed relief that Mac's sister Shanthee and her husband Lucky had come from Durban to stay with us to help me through this period. He had specifically asked that we tell them the truth, that Mac would be underground in South Africa.

Mac and I said our goodbyes to each other at home the next day, as I could not bear to go to the airport and risk crying in front of the children.

'When will you be back, Dad?' Milou asked wistfully as Mac was about to get into the car.

'I'm not so sure, son, it depends on when I get better. But I'll write to you all,' he said sadly as he held Milou to him.

An answer like 'next week' or 'next month' or even 'next year', something with a time limit, might have been easier to handle: there would be something to look forward to. But Mac wouldn't lie to them any more than he needed to. Even before the car drove off, Milou disappeared quietly into the house, while Joey clung to my side with her baby koala bear grip as we waved Mac off. As he disappeared from sight, I could only trust that we would not have to wait too long before seeing him again, and that the wait would not be too difficult. But at least we now had Lucky and Shanthee, who had come to be at our side.

Not long after, there was another attempt to break into this UN house too. But again, this time with the help of Lucky and Shanthee, we foiled the intruders. The break-in attempt that most traumatised Joey, however, was when I was reading the children a story in bed one night. Joey happened to glance at the mirror opposite my bed, only to see reflected in the glass the faces of three men peering at us through a small window halfway between the headboard and the ceiling. The image petrified her. Even today she sometimes refuses to draw her curtains closed at night, in case those faces are there, peering at her through the window!

*   *   *   *   *

'My necklace! Where is it?' I asked, greatly agitated as I fumbled around my neck to find it. 'And the matching earrings?' when I found my ears bare too.

'Don't worry, my dear,' the nurse said, looking down at me. 'We've locked them up safely.'

'What am I doing in hospital?' I asked, as I became aware of the drip in my arm. My head felt as if it had been in a tumble-dryer.

'You were brought in here thirty-six hours ago by a motorist who witnessed a serious road accident, in which you were involved. Do you remember anything?' the nurse asked.

'Only that I was on my way home from a UN gathering. I don't remember anything else,' I said, confused.

'Not to worry. You remember that you were wearing a necklace and earrings, so your mind must be intact,' the nurse reassured me.

I had been working flat out for a week, with virtually no sleep, on a report for Bax Nomvete – then head of the Preferential Trade Area – on the findings I had made at the United Nations Centre for Trade and Development in Geneva (UNCTAD/GATT), where I had just spent two weeks. On my return I gave Bax a verbal report that had greatly disturbed him, as I was completely candid about how certain officials in Geneva had been cutting huge corners in the design and development of the computer-based trade information system – to be used by the fourteen PTA member states – that we were jointly setting up. I was very unhappy about this and keen to finish the written report detailing these problems, as Bax wanted it by Friday 7 October 1988, in time for a meeting of the fourteen PTA representatives to be held in Lusaka that weekend.

As if this wasn't enough to keep me awake in the small hours, Ivan and Archie of Vula – who, like JS, had keys to my home and study, where I was working – would pop in even at two or three in the morning to send or collect messages on behalf of JS and OR. JS, too, would often arrive at odd hours of the day or night. Neither my home nor study felt like mine any more. I couldn't even take for granted the privacy needed to hang out all my underwear on a drying rack fitted in the study!

On completing my report on Friday 7 October, I was completely exhausted and wanted nothing more than to go home and relax with my children in a hot bubble bath, crawl into bed with them and read them all the stories they wanted to hear. But it was not to be.

Bax was having a dinner at his place that Friday evening for a few of the PTA representatives who had arrived in Lusaka early, for private discussions before the weekend meeting. He felt it very important that I show my face. I told Bax it would have to be very brief. He agreed.

I dashed home from work to tell the children I would have to go out briefly, and Joey noticed that I was wearing my 'serpent' sandals. She begged me to change footwear, saying the sandals looked evil. But my other sandals weren't as comfortable. As I drove towards the gate, both of them ran after the car, Joey still crying for me to stay with them.

'I'll be back within an hour,' I promised, by now as upset as the children.

At the corner I wanted to turn back, but my promise to my boss spurred me on.

'The sooner I get there, the sooner I'll be home,' I consoled myself as I pressed down hard on the accelerator.

I excused myself from the gathering within forty-five minutes of arriving and drove out of Bax's gate in the direction of my home. The next thing I knew, I woke up in hospital, thirty-six hours later. I must have fallen asleep or had a blackout at the wheel. That accident would have repercussions we could not imagine at the time.

I spent nine days in the University Teaching Hospital of Zambia in the burns unit because there were no beds left in the orthopaedic unit. And because the X-ray machine was not working properly, they could not determine the full extent of my injuries. The most obvious ones were all on my left side: a broken, dislocated shoulder, a smashed left collarbone and a severed upper arm bone. When I regained consciousness, a crèpe sling around my neck to support my arm and shoulder was the extent of the 'treatment' I had so far received.

'Zarina, wake up! You have some visitors,' Abdul Singh, a driver-cum-bodyguard of Mac's, whispered in my ear as he tugged gently on my good arm to rouse me.

Peering down at me were five men from the Transvaal and Natal Indian Congresses, delegates who had the previous day arrived in Lusaka for talks with the ANC. When told of my accident and that Mac was away, they had asked to see me. Delirious as I was from pain, one thing was crystal clear in my mind: don't let slip that Mac is in South Africa and not Moscow.

One member of the delegation, Jerry Coovadia, could not hide his concern at my condition. A prominent doctor himself – today in the vanguard of those in the medical fraternity struggling against AIDS in South Africa – he told me years later that he'd rated my chances of recovery very low. For one, he had taken my blood pressure before Abdul had woken me up and had found it to be dangerously low, and yet there was not a single doctor or senior nurse available that he could call for help.

Bax and his wife were equally appalled at my condition and the low level of care and hygiene at the hospital. Not able to walk, I had to crawl to the toilet on all fours when the nursing staff, not realising the extent of my injuries, refused to bring me a bedpan. Bax assured me that the UN doctors were working hard at getting me admitted somewhere else as soon as possible. When JS later came to the hospital, he was relieved that the UN and not Vula would have to organise better medical care for me. He told me that it was a matter of principle that the UN take care of me as their employee. But, he assured me, he would tell Mac of the accident and keep him informed of my progress.

It was well known that even in the processing of emergency accident cases like mine, the bureaucratically burdened UN could be grindingly slow. I could have been lying in the Lusaka hospital for weeks, waiting to be transferred. So I was disturbed, and puzzled, by JS's stance. It did not square with how much I knew he valued and appreciated my unconditional support of Mac's work. He had expressed this again when he was in Moscow, helping Mac and Gebuza complete their preparations to enter South Africa. Mac had even mentioned it in his letter of goodbye: '[JS] was in awe of your strength and bravery. He said to me, "Mac, Zarina is even braver than you. Do you know that?" While talking about you and your bravery he began to weep ...'

OR was not in Lusaka during this period and did not even know that I had been in an accident. The first Mac heard of it was ten days after it happened, fortuitously, when Ismail 'Momo' Momoniat, who was at Lusaka airport on his way back to Johannesburg, spotted me being pushed in a wheelchair by a Chinese UN doctor.

The doctor was taking me to Harare, where I would undergo major orthopaedic surgery. Momo alerted Mac to this immediately on his return to South Africa, where they were working together in the underground.

It transpired that JS had decided not to inform Mac of my accident. Perhaps he feared that such news might distract Mac from his work and so endanger Operation Vula. This wouldn't have surprised me, in light of a conversation I'd had with JS soon after Mac and Gebuza had entered South Africa. He had said that there are sacrificial lambs in all struggles, and that, like his own children and countless others in the struggle, that was sadly and unavoidably what Milou and Joey were!

* * * * *

The children came to see me on the Sunday I regained consciousness. To this day I can see the shock and dismay on their faces when they arrived at my bedside. If Jerry Coovadia and his TIC/NIC delegation, Bax and his wife, the Chimowitzes, Steve Tshwete, Zanele Mbeki, Jackie Molefe and my other visitors could not hide their shock at my condition, how could the children?

Joey greeted me, then crept under the bed, where she hid for the rest of the visit, refusing to come out till it was time to go. Milou spent most of the time trying to console and pacify her. On their way to the hospital they had apparently passed what was left of the Toyota I had wrapped around a tree. Noting the number plate was mine, Milou had tried to comfort Joey, who was convinced I was dead.

Even Steve Tshwete had concluded I couldn't have come out of that scrap alive. 'Mom is not dead, you'll see,' Milou reassured his sister.

But Joey wasn't convinced. She took a flower from the bunch she had collected from the garden for me and tried to guess my fate. Picking the first petal, she chanted, 'Mom won't die.' The next petal 'Mom will die.' Until the last petal told them I would die!

'Nonsense! But even if that happens, I'll become your mother and your father and your brother,' Milou promised her.

My heart bled for my children that day. It was one thing for their dad to have left for Moscow for medical treatment – that was the story we told everyone, including the children – but now their mom was sick too and would have to go away to get better. Fortunately Shanthee and Lucky were there from South Africa to try to help the children through this period.

By the time I reached the hospital in Harare ten days after the accident, I couldn't even lift my neck from the pillow to sip a glass of water. From then on I had to use a straw to drink. It later transpired that by now Mac was insisting on full medical reports so that he could assess for himself the extent and seriousness of my injuries. But he was never sent those reports, probably for the same reasons he had not been told of my accident for so long.

Even under local anaesthetic, I found the X-ray process excruciating. Once they had identified all nineteen fractures, including several rib and hairline spinal fractures, and the permanent damage to the shoulder cartilage, caused by the UN's bureaucratic delay in getting me to Harare, the medical staff nicknamed me 'Lady of Steel' for having come through ten days in such a state, untreated, fully conscious and with only Panado for the pain. They put this down to my regular jogs around Lusaka, and one doctor eventually confided that I might not have been able to walk again were it not for my fitness.

A month passed with no word from Mac.

'Why doesn't that so-and-so send me a message, ask me how I'm doing?' I would curse as I lay alone in Harare, thinking that he knew but was too busy to find the time to make contact. I understood that perhaps it was too risky to phone me at the hospital – I couldn't bring myself to believe that he would do this to me deliberately.

'He must be worried about the children, at least,' I would tell myself, struggling to understand but knowing what we meant to him. I recalled the words in his letter of goodbye: 'You are in my thoughts all the time, you and our glorious children ... How I miss you, love. How I miss Milou with his so gentle eyes, lying with his head on my lap, stroking my hand. Joey with her eyes alive, cuddling up to me ... I caress them with my heart ... [You] give me strength ... [My] pain is born of the passion of my love for you.'

Yet in all the weeks I was in Harare I didn't hear from him at all, not even a message. It turned out later that Mac's messages, which he had sent via Lusaka, had not reached me.

Once I started to walk again, two months after the accident, I sent for the children. The Christmas school holidays had arrived. While arranging with Ivan Pillay, who was in charge of Operation Vula's administration, that the children be sent to me, he admitted that Mac had not been sent my medical reports, nor had he been informed of the severity of my injuries. These had been played down. I realised then why Mac's messages were not reaching me. Had Mac and I communicated, he would have known the extent of my injuries, and they must have feared that his reaction might jeopardise Operation Vula.

The children and I moved into Bharat and Fatima's maid's quarters near the hospital, where I had to attend as an outpatient, but I still couldn't drive, shop, cook or keep house. Shanthee and Lucky had by now arranged to return to South Africa to attend to Lucky's own medical problems. That's when Pal Kadji, a Hungarian who had been teaching in Zimbabwe for five years, came to our rescue. Pal had been on the verge of marrying my sister when she called the wedding off.

Pal shopped, cooked, drove the children around and even sat me up in bed when necessary, as at that stage the injuries to my spine did not always allow me to do this by myself. His selfless help through that traumatic time remains unforgettable. When he returned to Masvingo at the beginning of the new school term in January 1989, I decided to go back to Lusaka with the children.

In preparation for my return I kept phoning my house, but for days and nights on end received no reply. What had happened to JS, Ivan and Archie, who I knew were using the place as a safe house? In the end I phoned my friend Marje Chimowitz in Lusaka to ask her to go to my home and find out what was going on.

When Marje got there, she rang the bell several times. Eventually, a young, attractive woman opened the door.

'What do you want?' she asked Marje in a strong foreign accent.

'Zarina is worried,' Marje said. 'She wants to know why nobody is answering her phone. She'll be back home in a few days' time.'

The woman said that all was fine, that she was living in the house with other comrades, and that Marje should reassure me that the phone was not being answered under strict instructions. But she didn't give Marje her name.

It turned out that, under JS and Ivan's instructions, the house had been completely taken over for clandestine work. Years later, Connie Braam of the Dutch Anti-Apartheid Movement, who had played a supporting role in Vula, told me it was she who had spoken to Marje at the gate, and that she was using the children's bedroom at the time, while Vula support staff occupied the other rooms in the house.

It was only after I returned to Lusaka in 1989, three months after my accident, that Mac and I were in touch again, via Tim's system. But he still hadn't received the medical reports he'd been asking for. As fate would have it, no sooner had I resettled the children into school than I developed a 'post-traumatic' cataract of the eye, which half blinded me. OR had just returned to Lusaka and wasted no time in arranging the best possible treatment for me in Moscow, at a renowned medical institute.

It did not even enter his mind that my health was the UN's responsibility. Such acts to bolster and nurture us – he would personally come to check on us whenever he could, once scolding me for Milou's torn pants and for letting him walk on our high security wall – revealed the importance he placed on the means as well as the ends of our struggle.

Again I had to leave the children.

Now OR approached the president of the Women's League, Ma Gertrude Shope, for help with the children. She appointed a young woman, Doris, to come and live with us to look after them. (Doris and I were to meet again in Johannesburg in 2004, when she told me that she too had named her son Amilcar.)

For some reason I believed I would be in Moscow for three weeks at the most. It turned out to be two months. During my stay, I met up with several of our students in Moscow, as well as our chief representative, Comrade Simon Makana, and Shubin, the Muscovite who was working closely with Mac, JS and OR in Operation Vula. He ensured that I was well taken care of, allotting me a monthly spending allowance in roubles.

I shared a hospital room with the mother of the prime minister of Afghanistan. We couldn't speak a common language but got on like a house on fire, communicating with hand gestures. Still, despite the general bonhomie of all the people I came into contact with, I was deeply upset by what these repeated and unexpected separations were doing to my children. My longing to be with them and keep them strong became overwhelming. Only by getting out of the hospital every afternoon and going for two- or three-hour-long walks along tracks cut through the deep snow could I shake off some of my sadness.

A Kurdish freedom fighter from Iraq, who spoke good English, began to join me on these walks. Soon we were talking about our families. When he realised that I spent my entire rouble allowance each week on just one phone call from a public phone box to Lusaka or to Tim Jenkin in London, he told me he had saved up his entire allowance as he had nothing to spend it on in hospital.

'I could lend you more roubles if you need them,' he offered.

'But I spend all mine, so I won't be able to pay you back,' I replied.

'Let's exchange addresses and keep in touch. You can pay me back one day,' he urged.

I couldn't resist the offer. Now I could phone the children in Lusaka and Tim too, if I wanted to get a message to Mac through him. Shubin must have been really puzzled about where I got the money from for these calls, which required me to go through the hospital's telephone operator, as I never told him about my Kurdish friend.

As it happens, in the upheaval of my eventual return to Lusaka, I lost his address. And, as I never received a letter from him, I was unable to repay his kind generosity.

Soon Shubin sent me to Yalta, in the Crimea, on the Black Sea, where Stalin, Churchill and Roosevelt had met for the Yalta Conference at the end of the Second World War. I was shown the room where they had signed the Yalta agreement, and even the table around which they'd sat. The sense of history in this room was very strong.

But the real purpose of my trip to Yalta was to visit the hospital where Mac was now supposed to be recuperating from his kidney disease, so that I could reinforce the legend that he was hospitalised on my return to Lusaka. His kidney disease was supposed to have worsened since his arrival in Moscow the year before. There was a valid reason for the Yalta deception. Shubin was very concerned that comrades passing through Moscow might ask to visit Mac in hospital. Such a request would be awkward to refuse and might blow his cover – unless Shubin could say he was recovering in Yalta, a destination out of reach of the comrades.

Shubin even ensured that postcards, which Mac had pre-written to me, were regularly posted in Moscow and Yalta c/o the ANC office, Lusaka, as if he were really in the Soviet Union. These postcards, informing me of the progress of his 'treatment' and enquiring after us, did a lot to perpetuate the legend and keep the police off his tracks in South Africa.

Soon after my return to Lusaka, I had to go back to Harare to have the steel pin removed from my arm, and yet another operation to try to fix my dislocated shoulder. When even this second operation failed, my boss Bax Nomvete approached the UN to send me to Harley Street, London, to try to get my health sorted out so that I could start working again. It was now April/May 1989, six months since the accident. I had by now submitted my claim to the UN headquarters in New York for compensation for the service-incurred injuries and shoulder disfigurement I had suffered. Yet they still agreed to send me, accompanied by the children, to London for further medical treatment entirely at their expense.

When I told Mac via the underground communications system

that London would be my next stop, he replied that he would try to meet us there, once he had debriefed OR and JS in Moscow. His main problem now would be slipping undetected out of South Africa to the Soviet Union. Once in London, he would say that he had been discharged from hospital for the time being.

We arrived in London on 21 July 1989. Tim took us from the airport straight to the flat he had found for us near Regent's Park. Mac was supposed to arrive that day, but didn't make it. We had to wait another week for him to appear.

I still had a lot of pain in my back, neck, shoulder and arm, so I wore the arm sling for relief whenever possible. Both the children had long been looking after themselves as much as they could, but that week, on a couple of occasions when we were out walking in Regent's Park, Joey's knees or ankles would suddenly seize up and I would have to carry her home. She was later to be admitted to a paediatric hospital in Sussex for this condition.

Milou grew even quieter than usual that week, once asking if I really believed Mac would have the time to visit us in London. He had overheard Archie tell Ivan that, for his dad to have gone away like that, he must really love his country more than his family. I was extremely angry about Archie's insensitive remark. I tried as best I could to remind Milou and make him understand that his dad truly loved us, that he drew his strength from us and that if he had had any choice, he would not have gone away.

'It's *because* he loves us so much that he is fighting for a better life for us at home,' I repeated once more.

I think my words were beginning to ring hollow to him. Until then I had no idea that he had heard Archie's remark, bottled it up and was trying to deal with this too.

A self-contained child, Milou had shown maturity beyond his years. I first noticed his capacity to fend for himself and try to help us through difficult situations when he was just four years old. He got lost on a jam-packed beach in Bournemouth and, after a massive hunt by security, was assumed kidnapped by 'paedophiles' – some older boys he, his sister and Maya had earlier been playing with in the sea.

In fact, he'd somehow got lost in the crowd when he came out of the water. On realising this, he started to look for the distant, crowded car park, and then searched through the masses of cars for the one we had arrived in. He managed to find the car and waited there even as it grew dark – wearing only a swimming costume and shivering with cold – knowing we'd have to come back to the car once we'd given up the hunt for him.

When he was thirteen, he saved his sister and me from an insidious ocean current that kept sweeping our boat back to where we had started each time we struggled to row back to the mainland. This went on for hours. When we didn't show up for afternoon tea, Milou got worried and came looking for us in another rowing boat. He immediately saw what the problem was and worked out a way he could row back to shore, beating the current. Following his plan, he was able to reach landfall and call for a motorboat to come and rescue us.

But we had completely misread Milou's ability to think problems through to their practical solution, assuming that once he accepted that there were good reasons for Mac's absence and our painful circumstances, he would somehow feel it less. How unfair of so many of us in the struggle to have expected so much of our children, when even adults often cannot reconcile emotionally what they rationally know must be done.

I decided then that if OR and JS had instructed Mac in Moscow to return to his post in South Africa, I would not go back to Zambia. For one, the PTA job would require my total focus and lots of travel, and even my role as breadwinner could no longer justify leaving the children in the care of others again, especially now that I had accumulated sufficient savings to quit working for a while. And I was still in need of good medical treatment. As a British citizen, I could stay on in the UK.

On 27 July, Tim confirmed that Mac would be arriving the next day, having been promised a visa by the British Consulate in Moscow. Milou excitedly asked to go for a haircut and had his hair gelled back stylishly. It made him look older than his seven years.

At the airport, waiting in the international arrivals hall, we could see Mac through the glass doors in intense conversation with the immigration officials. Part of his recent disguise, a big, dyed Afro perm, was gone, and his moustache and goatee were growing back. Thank God his hair was not blond, I thought, recalling the words in his letter: 'Got involved in intensive preparations esp[ecially] in disguises. It was decided to bleach my natural hair. Have already had six bleachings – it's now yellow blond but they are confident they'll get it right. Big improvement on wigs as it gives greater flexibility, less bothersome (after this bleaching will have to be about once a month) and with wigs gives variations. Outside of one visit to a concert – it's all work, work and work. But that's good as it helps to concentrate my mind.'

He was dressed in a business suit and tie. His body language did not look good at all, but thankfully he was allowed through in the end, the last one from the Moscow flight. We had last seen him one year, three weeks and three days ago! So much had happened since then that we were all at a loss for words.

Mac took the children out to play in nearby parks every day, even when I had no physiotherapy or other medical appointments. When a week had passed, he mentioned that OR and JS had arranged a three-week holiday for our family on the Black Sea. We could take the holiday once my treatment in London had run its course towards the end of August 1989, and before his return to his underground post in South Africa.

I made a point of not contacting anybody in England that week, especially as Mac might soon have to return to South Africa, and no one I knew, except Tim and Joel Joffe in Swindon, who'd funded Vula at its initial stages, were aware of what he had really been up to. And what if Mac didn't look like someone who'd just recently been dying of a kidney disease?

As it was now only six weeks to the beginning of the new school year, I suggested that it would be better for the family if we skipped the Black Sea and instead used the coming weeks to check out schools for the children and a place at a university for me.

Partly through my personal experiences I had become passionate about gender and development issues, and hoped to gain admission somewhere, even at this late stage, to a master's degree. With Bax's eventual blessing I formally resigned from the PTA and never went back to Lusaka again. Instead we moved into a campus flat at Sussex University in October 1989. Mac and the kids went back to Lusaka to pack up the house and to settle some outstanding debts not long after I started my course at the Institute of Development Studies.

When they returned around November 1989, the children started school near campus. But because of the racist abuse Milou in particular was experiencing at the school, we took them out during the Christmas break, having moved off-campus close to the Balfour Road Primary School in Brighton, where they were to start in January 1990. That same month Mac returned to South Africa, although 'officially' he was being readmitted to hospital.

Some months after Mac's return to the underground, Madiba, who was released from prison in February 1990, advised Mac to exit South Africa, and re-enter legally under an indemnity from prosecution given to all ANC leaders. In yet another disguise he went to India, and from there arrived in Sussex, supposedly after the successful treatment of his illness in the Soviet Union.

Mac spent one day and night with us before re-entering South Africa legitimately in June 1990, under the pretext that he hadn't been in the country since he escaped from house arrest in 1977, following his release from Robben Island.

Ironically, once lawfully in South Africa, Mac was soon arrested, having avoided capture by the security apparatus when he was in the country illegally and underground! His arrest followed those of his Vula colleagues Pravin Gordhan, Billy Nair and Siphiwe Nyanda (Gebuza).

That was when Valli phoned us in July 1990, informing us that Mac had been arrested.

CHAPTER 10

Freedom, be humane!

JOZI

'We can't make it to your wedding, sorry, *neef*, I'm under a police order restricting me to the magisterial district of Johannesburg.' Mac was on the phone to one of his nephews, who was getting married in Durban around Christmas 1990, and wanted us to attend. We had just arrived in South Africa a week before, on 19 December, and were staying in the home of UDF comrades in Mayfair, who were away on holiday.

Having been charged with terrorism in late November, along with other Vula operatives who had been arrested, Mac was now out on R180 000 bail. It must have been through the sheer excitement of finally being back together in Jozi – a prospect that had for so long seemed so remote – and the ongoing negotiations between the ANC and De Klerk's government, that I clung to the belief that the Vula trial would be dropped before it could start in mid-January 1991, especially given the indemnity from prosecution under which Mac had returned home. Right now we were simply soaking up the ecstasy of our family reunion, momentously on our very own South African soil!

'Will you really have to go on trial again, Dad?' Milou asked as the trial date drew nearer. 'Will you be going back to prison?' He was really worried.

'What's terrorism?' asked Joey.

Now that we had explained to them why Mac had been inside South Africa, what he had been trying to do under the leadership of Uncle OR and Uncle JS, and why we'd had to tell them he was in Moscow, they were even more confused.

'But if Dad was doing what the ANC had told him to do and apartheid wants to make friends with the ANC, why don't they all make friends with Dad?'

Milou had overheard my conversations with the media outside South Africa House in London, in which I'd mentioned that Mac had returned to South Africa legally when ANC leaders had been invited to do so.

'Then why is he still going on trial, Ma?' Milou asked, puzzled. 'Will he be tortured again?'

During Mac's recent imprisonment, the police had been bent on getting Mac to talk. They wanted to know who in apartheid's own structures had been working with Vula, where all the weapons were stored and where the rest of the safe houses were. Mac's interrogators assaulted him in an attempt to get answers to these questions. Once Mac told Madiba of the physical abuse, he warned Basie Smit, the Deputy Commissioner of Police, to stop it immediately, but not before it landed Mac in St Aidan's hospital in Durban as a result of the existing problem with his neck.

Now that Mac was out on bail, we were hopeful that, in terms of the so-called Pretoria Minute, which endorsed the end of all political trials, the Vula trial would be called off. Madiba had apparently kept on pressing De Klerk to release Mac and his colleagues from prison, and now to get the trial quashed. But Mac was later to learn from certain of the ANC's NEC members, who at the time were party to the NEC discussions about the fate of the Vula operatives, that the attempts of Madiba, Walter Sisulu, JS and others to get them released as soon as possible received little support from some other NEC members. We discovered this after the NEC had released a press statement confirming that Vula was an ANC operation. Now their attitude was simply to leave them locked up.

'Let them swing,' was by all accounts the gist of their message. 'If we were the government, we'd do just that.'

These same comrades continued to spread the rumour that Vula was a maverick operation not authorised by the ANC, despite the press release to the contrary.

This anger and hostility towards the Vula team would have made more sense if its underground activities – revealed when the police stumbled on certain records after Mac's legal return to South Africa – actually posed a threat to the negotiations for a peaceful settlement.

Still, the denialists within the movement's leadership grew more vocal. One could understand this reaction from those who had been excluded from knowing about the operation because of OR's resolute refusal to divulge anything about it to the NEC – several of whom came to know of it only after Mac's arrest.

But it later came to light that those who were the angriest and most vociferous in renouncing Vula had actually been told, by JS, of both the operation and Mac's internal command before Mac had even left Lusaka to take up his underground post in South Africa! So they could hardly be upset about having been left out of the loop.

What then would explain their persistent denials? I believe those in the movement who considered Mac to be 'arrogant' saw his reputation and his position as a threat. There was, perhaps, an unspoken agreement among these comrades to 'bring Mac down'. If this was the case, why didn't anyone in the Lusaka leadership who knew about Mac's involvement in Vula volunteer to replace or join him inside South Africa if they were against his leading the operation? It certainly would have made our lives a lot easier!

In Mac's letter of goodbye, he mentioned the great difficulty of the task ahead of us: 'I feel the immense weight on my shoulders. In a sense even Sylvester [deputy commander of Vula] begins to look to me. Your presence by my side and the knowledge that our family, as family, a single unit is going into battle and not me as an individual, gives me great courage ... Hence I feel a sense of guilt about the welter of unsorted details that I left you with. You have an immense task even without them.'

These political undercurrents were developing into a dangerous deluge that could easily have drowned the weak among us, but, fortunately for all, the trial against the Vula activists – who included Gebuza, Pravin Gordhan and Billy Nair – was eventually quashed, thanks mainly to the pressure Madiba put on De Klerk, the alliance made up of the ANC, the SACP and COSATU, which mobilised their grassroots membership to call for Mac's release, and demands from the international community. But not before we had attended some of the court hearings in Durban, which had started on 15 January 1991.

Finally our family could move out of the limbo in which the terrorism charges had kept us trapped. We could now finally make some concrete plans.

We found a home of our own in Yeoville in Johannesburg. Joey, captivated by the novelty of the four of us living under one roof again, decided that South Africa was definitely where she wanted to be. This in spite of her still conflicting feelings towards Mac – on the one hand she felt angry with him for his long absences, when he was never there for her, and on the other a deep pride for his role in the struggle, and the loyalty and boldness with which he had carried out his part.

Milou, who was also grappling with ambivalent emotions, felt that his place was with his father. We believed and hoped that time would help them understand and reconcile their conflicting feelings as part of the healing process.

Mac and I were relieved that we would not have to try to talk the children into remaining in South Africa. We enrolled them at the nearby non-racial Sacred Heart Primary School. I resumed work on my IDS assignments, which I had stopped following Mac's arrest, and which would qualify me to write my master's thesis. On the face of it, our lives were now coming together.

Then, out of the blue, in mid-1991, bold headlines appeared in a couple of newspapers stating that Mac was planning to assassinate Madiba, apparently in an attempt to destabilise the ANC. The

Citizen newspaper, a government mouthpiece and apologist for apartheid, led this story with particular gusto.

A Mozambican called Cunha, who in fact had been working with the security forces, is supposed to have admitted under questioning that Mac had met with him at our home to hatch several plots. Mac denied this, or that he even knew the man.

The *Citizen* reporters came along to photograph our home. When I refused the photographers entry, they took photos of the outside of the house through our front gate, which had the house number clearly displayed on it. They also took pictures of my old Toyota Conquest and number plate, which were visible through the gate. When Mac arrived home later, I tried to warn him off by shouting through a window that there were snoopers around, but they got photos of him, his car and the number plate. They published the full details of our cars and address in their paper. They even used my refusal to let them enter our house and the fact that I'd warned Mac when he arrived home to insinuate Mac's guilt in the Cunha fabrications!

The Goldstone Commission on Violence found Cunha to be a liar and his allegations regarding Mac to be without substance.

By now our home address – 27 Muller Street, Yeoville – our number plates, and the colour and make of our cars were public knowledge, at a time when South Africa's *verkrampte* enemies of change were determined to eliminate the ANC leadership.

And we were catching flak from both sides. On the one hand, Mac's own colleagues seemed to want to cut him down to size for reasons known only to themselves. On the other hand, forces within the security establishment seemed determined to destroy him.

*　*　*　*　*

It was now April 1991. The Vula trial had been called off the month before. Mac had gone to support the children at Sacred Heart Primary School's annual swimming gala. They spent all morning at the gala and had a lot of fun. Then, as they drove home afterwards, a cloud of black smoke suddenly began to billow from the car's bonnet. Mac immediately switched off the car and left it on the roadside. He contacted some comrades to come and remove what they believed was a crude bomb attached to the engine. The bomb must have been planted while they were at the gala, and could have detonated with the children in the car.

Joey phoned me in England, where I'd been for four weeks to tie up loose ends, to tell me about the bomb. Mac, however, encouraged me to stay and finish what I was doing rather than rush back. Everything was fine, he reassured me. They may have only four plastic chairs, a plastic table, a small pot, a pan and two mattresses, but they loved it, even though they ate mainly fish fingers and boiled peas for supper, which was all Mac cooked most of the time!

Not long after I got home, Marius Schoon telephoned me from the Kahns' house across from ours, where he was visiting. Marius was a friend and comrade from the late seventies, whose wife Jeannette and six-year-old daughter Katryn had been blown to pieces in front of his three-year-old son Fritz by a parcel bomb in the kitchen of their home in exile in Angola. The man who had sent the bomb, Craig Williamson, was a security police spy who had pretended to be their friend, and had once even stayed with them. He had also sent the parcel bomb that had killed Ruth First.

Marius, who had served twelve years in Pretoria Central Prison for his stand against the apartheid regime, would later oppose Williamson's application for amnesty during the Truth and Reconciliation Commission. Like the eminent Bram Fischer, Marius too had been labelled a *verraaier* (traitor) by apartheid's protagonists. Yet the majority of South Africans – the black oppressed and all progressive whites – hailed these men as 'the original anti-apartheid Afrikaners'.

Now Marius phoned to warn me that a huge, balding white man had just jumped over our wall from inside our yard and run off at great speed towards a waiting car. Mac was away for the weekend at a highly publicised ANC conference. That night I got another telephone call.

'You f***ing bitch, we know your husband's away tonight, so we're coming to get you,' someone ranted in a heavy Afrikaans accent.

Before he could continue, I hung up, but then heard a sound outside my front door. Terrified, I tried to reach Marius and Yusuf Mahomed, but they weren't answering. Fortunately the curtains were all closed, so at least I wasn't visible as I tried to make more phone calls.

The sound of footsteps prowling the narrow lanes around the house continued. As I searched for the telephone number of ANC Security, the phone rang again. It was the same abusive man who had called earlier.

'ANC Security are on their way to my house right now,' I lied. 'They won't have difficulty tracing you through your telephone number.'

He hung up, and within moments I heard talking outside, as if on a walkie-talkie, then a heavy thud and footsteps, as if someone had jumped the wall and was now running away down the pavement. I tried to compose myself. If these people were so easily frightened off, they couldn't be that serious about hurting me; maybe all they wanted was to scare me. Thankfully Joey and Milou had slept through everything.

Not long after that incident, I noticed a stranger, an African man, sitting on the corner of our block, or sometimes diagonally across from our front gate, eating sandwiches or reading a newspaper. It was obvious that he was watching our movements.

One afternoon, after I'd collected the children from school, the electricity happened to be off and my remote control wouldn't open the gate. I had to leave the children in the car while I climbed over the gate to open it manually from the inside, and, suddenly, for the first time, the man's presence really got to me. I could feel his eyes piercing the back of my head like lasers as I climbed over the gate.

'We're sitting ducks,' I thought. 'They could kill any one of us at this gate if they wanted to.'

By mid-1992, a 'hit' list, rumoured to have been drawn up by extreme right-wingers intent on thwarting the forces of progressive change, was supposedly circulating in right-wing circles. This list apparently included the names of Chris Hani, Joe Slovo and Mac. We now felt extremely unsafe in Yeoville, and in February 1993 moved to a house in nearby Observatory, where proper burglar bars, adequate outside lighting and a security alarm system were urgently installed by the ANC.

By now the bloodletting and violence in the country, aimed at derailing the negotiations and portrayed mainly as 'black-on-black' violence in townships, villages and on commuter trains, had intensified. Covertly instigated by and directly involving apartheid agents from the police and military establishment to forestall the negotiations and destabilise the country, this was in fact the work of a 'third force', made up of extreme reactionaries bent on preserving white privilege.

Shortly after our move to Observatory, Mac was appointed joint secretary – with Fanie van der Merwe, his National Party counterpart – of the multiparty negotiation process, known as the Convention for a Democratic South Africa (CODESA). This did not go down well at all with his detractors, who had been portraying him as an ANC 'hawk' because of Vula.

In his capacity as joint secretary of the multiparty negotiations, Mac was provided with ANC bodyguards, and not a moment too soon. On 10 April 1993, just as CODESA was kicking off, Chris Hani was assassinated in his driveway.

Mac, Milou and Joey were visiting his niece Madhuri in Stanger on the day of Hani's assassination. They had left the previous evening, to allow me to focus on meeting my deadline at the end of April for the submission of my master's thesis.

On the Saturday afternoon of Hani's assassination, officials from ANC Security arrived at our house in Observatory and told me that I would have to leave for a while. They feared for my safety.

'I'll be fine here, honestly,' I pleaded with them.

I really couldn't face moving any more, not even temporarily. As a compromise, Security got hold of Sam, one of Mac's bodyguards, to come and stay with me until Mac returned.

It was soon revealed that the police had found a hit list in the getaway car of Hani's assassin, Janus Walusz. Chris Hani's name had indeed been on that list, as had Mac's and Joe Slovo's. So the earlier rumours of a hit list were indeed true. Thank God we took them seriously! Walusz and his right-wing backers were intending to go on a killing spree aimed at their most hated enemies.

Milou and Joey, who watched the news and learnt of the hit list, were upset and more fearful now than ever before for their dad's safety. They felt the pain of Chris's children deeply, especially the daughter who had watched her father being killed. Grateful that their dad was spared this fate, vigilance now became Milou and Joey's watchword.

The work at the World Trade Centre, the main venue for the negotiations, was all-absorbing, and once again we saw little of Mac. But at whatever unearthly hour he arrived from work, he was home every night, and that made all the difference.

In September 1993, Milou, now aged eleven, was playing on his friend's verandah that overlooked the street and our front gate. It was about 8 p.m. and quite dark. A car pulled up and parked outside his friend's house, opposite our gate, and turned its lights off. Milou edged towards the fence near to where the car was parked and could see the silhouettes of four people inside. As Mac's car drew up, ready to turn into our gate, which was already opening by remote control, Mac and his driver saw Milou screaming and gesticulating frantically from the verandah not to turn into our driveway. He shouted that there were people in the parked car. Mac's car immediately sped away past our gate, and by the time it returned, the other car had left. I am convinced that Milou had saved his dad from what could have been an assassination attempt.

During that period, the children and I were watching TV one evening. Suddenly footage appeared of the World Trade Centre as it was being stormed by the AWB, an extreme right-wing Afrikaner militant group led by a fanatical white supremacist, Eugene Terreblanche.

Intent on derailing the negotiations, Terreblanche and his cohorts had driven an armoured vehicle through the glass walls of the WTC, a shattering sight! Once inside, they ran through the place as if possessed, guns at the ready, looking for the negotiators and their personnel, whom they had threatened to take out.

It was quite frightening watching them go on the rampage, especially as we had to wait on tenterhooks, not knowing whether they would find any of the negotiators or their staff. Luckily, the negotiators' own bodyguards and the WTC's security officers had made the team barricade themselves into offices and take cover.

At times like these, when their anxiety was palpable, we reassured Milou and Joey that the enemies of change were growing weaker, had less resolve than the forces of progress and would lose their battle. Once a democratically elected government was in place – and this was now unstoppable – many of those hankering after the past would gradually adapt to the new order and set their sights ahead. Then such assaults as we had been witnessing on the well-being of those working for positive change would become a thing of the past. We would soon be approaching the harmony, peace and stability that had been eluding us, we assured them.

Because we truly believed that.

*   *   *   *   *

In November 1993, I applied and was interviewed for the position of senior gender researcher at the Centre for Applied Legal Studies (CALS) at the University of the Witwatersrand. The interview went well and we agreed that I would start working in early 1994.

The work was stimulating, as it involved investigating, among other things, a whole range of the apartheid government's laws and policies from the perspective of gender sensitivity.

I was just settling into the job when, following South Africa's first ever democratic elections on 27 April 1994, which brought the ANC-led Government of National Unity to power, President Nelson Mandela appointed Mac Minister of Transport in his cabinet. We were delighted.

Now we needed to decide where we, as a family, should be based: Johannesburg or Cape Town? When parliament was not sitting in Cape Town for half the year, cabinet ministers would have to work from their government offices in Pretoria, so either we could move between the two cities with Mac every six months, which was not an option because of schooling, or be prepared to live apart from him for half the year, in whichever city we made our base.

In the end, especially as Milou had just started high school, we decided to remain in Joburg rather than start all over again in the Groote Schuur compound in Cape Town, which houses the president, cabinet ministers and parliamentarians. Joey too had just changed schools and I was in an interesting job.

So we agreed that Mac would commute between his work and home as his time allowed, living with us in Johannesburg whenever he could. Many MPs' families had to make this sort of compromise.

Not only had I not anticipated Mac's appointment to cabinet, I had hardly expected the social demands that would be placed on me as the wife of a prominent politician. For example, I would often have to accompany him to official state functions in South Africa and elsewhere.

In the early days of the new democratic government, Madiba invited us to join him on a memorable state visit to England, and we experienced at first hand Queen Elizabeth's affection for our leader. For example, Madiba was the first ever guest in Western attire who was not required to wear the customary black coat-tails and tie at a royal banquet (he came in a Madiba shirt). Another evening, at the Royal Albert Hall, he even got the queen to join him in a jive to the sounds of a South African band!

Respecting the protocol of our hosts, we were plunged into the pomp and pageantry of the occasion. Like Madiba, his daughter Zenani and the rest of the delegation, we even stayed in Buckingham Palace, something I could not have imagined would ever happen when, as a teenager living in London, I used to stand outside those palace gates and taunt the stern-looking guards with provocative comments!

When my duties as a cabinet minister's wife started requiring too much time off work, which would inevitably frustrate the schedules and targets I had set myself at CALS, I decided it would be best all round for me to resign. Instead I would resume writing from home, at least until I'd eased into the new situation and established a more reliable network of family support. Now that Mac was earning a salary for the first time since I'd met him, I could happily make this choice.

Mac worked in both Pretoria and Cape Town and travelled back and forth between the two cities constantly. He tried to come home most weekends. In 1996, when the family had more or less settled into this routine, I was ready to take on full-time work again. Several highly respected women in the National Executive Committee of the ANC – including some UDF veterans – nominated me for one of the gender commissioner posts in the statutory Commission for Gender Equality, which was to be set up shortly by government.

The interviewing panel, all female MPs, included a significant majority of ANC members, one Democratic Party member, one National Party member, and a representative or two from other parties, such as Inkatha and the African Christian Democratic Party.

On my way from Cape Town airport to parliament for the interview, I received a call on my cellphone from a cabinet minister.

'Don't go to that interview,' he said. 'I'll make you a director on the Diamond Board instead.'

Puzzled, and certainly not interested in sitting on the Diamond Board, I responded that my interest was in gender, and that I would be going ahead and attending the interview.

At the appointed time, the panel of interviewers called me in. I found their questions around gender transformation in South Africa fairly straightforward and reasonably easy to answer. In that sense the interview went very well for me. But two weeks later I was turned down for the job, with no explanations given. When some of those who had nominated me asked why I hadn't been successful, the leader of the ANC panellists told them that I had hopelessly failed the interview. Unable to believe this, they quietly asked other members of the panel how I'd fared.

'She was among the most impressive of the interviewees,' was the response. 'But we were outvoted. The matter of who was to be appointed as gender commissioners appears to have been decided long before any interviews were even held.'

Clearly, the interviews had been just a formality, and the offer of a Diamond Board directorship was meant to save the panel any embarrassment should questions be asked. Here was a case of jobs for pals if ever there was one and, being Mac's wife, I certainly was no pal.

Interestingly, at a state banquet for a visiting head of state two or three weeks later, many people told me how shocked they were to see me there. They had heard that I was seriously ill in hospital, where I would be recovering for some time. Putting two and two together, I figured that this rumour had been spread to explain why I could not be offered a job on the Gender Commission!

Similar things happened later, when prominent ANC figures recommended me for other jobs in the development field – all of which I was well qualified and well suited to do. The panel vetting applicants would not agree.

By now I had started writing an opinion column in a reputable newspaper on issues of gender and development in the context of South Africa's transformation. The editors had stipulated that they wished to attract a new, young, black female readership, with about three years of high-school education, who would be interested in South African women's issues in a global context. They wanted the column to be written in the simplest terms possible.

This challenge, combined with my part-time consultancy work with private-sector companies keen to start implementing empowerment programmes for women and blacks, provided me with a platform for stimulating research and the exchange of ideas.

When Mac retired from government in 1999 – the same year Madiba stepped down and Thabo Mbeki became president – I was drawn into a women-run business, while continuing my column and consultancy. Out of the blue, at the beginning of 2001, I received a fax from a woman closely linked to the highest echelons in government. She had been very influential in the appointments of people in the development field, and now she asked me to apply for a position as gender commissioner, which had just fallen vacant.

She told me when I contacted her that she was really impressed by the amount of research that had gone into my columns, and with my Women's Day keynote address to the Professional Women's League of KwaZulu-Natal, which had been circulated on the Internet. But I was puzzled by the reason for her change in attitude, as I knew she was aware, from the outset, of my capabilities in this field.

By now I didn't actually want the job, as the political intrigues surrounding my initial application and my subsequent applications for other jobs in the development field, which I had been asked to make, had put me off completely. So I did not bother to apply.

Meanwhile, Mac had joined the First Rand Bank as a board director. Shortly before, a senior cabinet minister had tracked us down on holiday to offer Mac the chairmanship of the Development Bank of Southern Africa, an offer that, as it happened, never materialised. Other opportunities offered to him fizzled out too, even though *Infrastructure Finance*, a leading New York journal, had selected him as one of eight government officials around the world who had been the 'most innovative and forward-thinking in their approach to privatisation and infrastructure development'.

A pattern was clearly emerging: prominent ANC figures were recommending us for certain positions for which we were well suited, then they were blocked by others from making it happen. We were being deliberately and systematically marginalised. Mac was finally being put in his proper place.

But not quite yet. He remained on the board of directors of First Rand, one of the most prestigious banks in the country.

One evening, at a cocktail party, a virulent detractor of Mac's was overheard saying about him, 'I will bring him down.'

*   *   *   *   *

As the children grew older, they made their peace with Mac, and enjoyed the 'normality' of a more settled family life than they'd ever had. Their earlier resentment towards him had given way to a deepening respect for and pride and pleasure in his past as political prisoner and freedom fighter.

As Joey once told us, as she got to know Mac, she was able to reconcile being the daughter who needed a loving father with the daughter whose father had chosen the struggle *instead* of her. As she came to understand exactly what he'd been fighting for and protecting her from, she realised he had chosen the struggle *because* of her and her brother. As Mac had written in his letter: 'Our beliefs, our commitment to doing whatever the struggle demands of us, become personal – intensely – because in concrete terms we seek to build a liveable life for the Joeys and the Milous … How even more glorious it would be [if] we had before then carved a society that grants us all a liveable life!'

'When I reached this turning point in my life,' Joey said, 'not only did I forgive him, I became happy to have shared him with other South Africans. Now I am in awe of him for paying the greatest tribute a father can give his child: to make a better life for her, or die trying.'

Joey even wrote Mac little notes about her feelings. Their gist was simply: 'We walk with our heads held high. Thank you.'

On the Sunday morning of 16 February 2003, as Joey cheerfully greeted us and sat down to join us for breakfast, she spotted the front-page headlines of the *Sunday Times*: 'Shaik paid money to Maharaj'. As Joey read the article, which we had already seen, she grew paler. The article insinuated that, during his tenure as Transport Minister, Mac had awarded two tenders worth billions of rands to consortia involving Schabir Shaik, a South African businessman, in exchange for payments. The 'payments' from Shaik were listed in great detail, their timing supposedly indicating that the awarding of the tenders had been in exchange for Shaik's money.

'Is this true, Dad?' Joey looked Mac in the eye.

'I was never bribed, my child,' he assured her. 'These allegations of corruption are false, believe me.'

Mac and I had been shocked at the slurs in the article, a shock deepened by the fact that a *Sunday Times* journalist, Jessica Bezuidenhout, had called Mac on the Friday afternoon – Valentine's Day – to inform him that they were considering running the article on the Sunday. She also wanted to ask Mac some questions. Mac asked her for a few days in which to gather evidence relevant to the issues she was raising. We believed we would be given this time.

It was clear that only the National Prosecuting Authority (NPA) could have fed this slanderous story to the *Sunday Times* – unlawfully, as it happened, in terms of the NPA Act. Tellingly, it transpired that this 'news' had been leaked to the *Sunday Times* by the NPA at a time when the NPA was in possession of conclusive documentary evidence, rigorously and painstakingly gathered by their investigative wing, the Scorpions, since February 2002, contradicting their own story!

The evidence amassed by them was that the State Tender Board and the National Roads Agency, both autonomous authorities totally independent of the Department of Transport, had respectively evaluated the relevant tender bids in terms of strict criteria, and awarded the tenders, on this basis, to the consortia in which Shaik had an interest; that Mac neither could have influenced, nor could have been involved in, nor was involved in either of their decisions; that the Department of Transport's own earlier evaluation and recommendation to the State Tender Board that it award the driver's licence tender to a consortium that was a rival of Shaik's was rejected by the State Tender Board, which asked the Director-General of Transport to weight the criteria differently and re-evaluate the tenders in terms of this new weighting; and that in terms of this new evaluation the consortium in which Shaik had an interest won the tender.

So the question is glaring: If there was no link between any payments made by Shaik to Mac and the awarding of the tenders to Shaik, and the NPA had conclusive proof of this, who was behind the leak to the press, and why?

Still reeling from the viciousness of the *Sunday Times* attack, Joey accompanied Mac to Woolworths later that morning. Hand in hand they did some shopping for her college lunch the next day. Joey had just started university, where she was meeting new people. The shop assistants flocked around Mac to greet him, as they often did. Though now retired from government and the leadership of the ANC – he preferred to be an ordinary rank-and-file ANC member – he was as popular as ever on the ground.

As they went to pay, Joey saw the stack of *Sunday Times* newspapers piled up near the tills, the lead article loudly denouncing Mac's integrity. She wished those headlines away, but they stared back at her. Suddenly she found herself slipping her hand out of Mac's in sheer embarrassment and humiliation. She could not face being seen as party to this 'crime'. Like the victim of a rape, *she* felt guilty and ashamed of this brutal violation of her family's dignity.

On the Monday after the *Sunday Times* article appeared, one of the authors of the article, Mzilikazi Wa Afrika, was interviewed live just after 8 a.m. on SAfm radio by John Perlman. In the interview, Wa Afrika astonishingly admitted, among other things, the following:

> Ah, firstly we are trying to find a connection between why Mr Maharaj was paid this kind of money, because we are not sure yet, but we got some ideas but we need to verify whether those ideas are true or not. But all we know is that Mr Maharaj was paid this money. But so far we are still trying to find out what for.

He also declared:

> You see we are not saying that awarding of those tenders, that is the R2.5 billion tender to upgrade the N3 road between Johannesburg and Durban and the one for the driver's licence, there's something wrong with that.

It is mind-boggling that the *Sunday Times*, on the very day after publishing the article alleging that Mac had accepted bribes from Shaik, conceded that they did not know whether such allegations were true or not; and, moreover, that they were not saying there had been any wrongdoing in the awarding of those tenders. Why then had they published an article so denigrating to us in the first place?

And the NPA continued to conduct 'further investigations' into Mac's 'corruption' as Minister of Transport between 1994 and 1999, despite knowing for a fact that he had not awarded those tenders.

We fully expected that these dirty tricks against us would continue. As they did. A black editor, Jovial Rantao, phoned Mac for his comments about my impending 'arrest' for tax evasion after newspapers had carried this story. Mac asked Rantao where he had got his information from, and we recorded his answer on tape: he had heard it from a 'reliable' source from within the Scorpions just a couple of weeks earlier.

Significantly, Bulelani Ngcuka, head of the Scorpions, had briefed black editors at around the same time. Was this another instance of the media being manipulated into attacking us?

The leaks to the media put the onus on Mac to prove his innocence in the court of world public opinion, instead of his accusers trying to prove his guilt in a court of law. Keeping him under this cloud of negative public opinion would serve their purpose of ruining his reputation, given that they knew full well they would not be able to convict him of corruption in a court of law.

We were particularly disgusted that these leaks to the media by the Scorpions and the contents of the briefing of the editors by Bulelani Ngcuka were in direct contravention of the law that governed the Scorpions and the NPA. In terms of this law, anyone found guilty of such leaks can be sentenced to up to fifteen years in prison. We were struck by the impunity with which the Scorpions were abusing their powers.

Following the *Sunday Times* article, a journalist asked Mac whether Bulelani Ngcuka, the head of the NPA, had been investigated in 1989/90 by ANC intelligence, and what the findings of the investigation had been. Mac confirmed openly and publicly that an investigation had indeed taken place and that, at the time, Intelligence had found that Ngcuka probably was a spy for the apartheid regime.

As a result, President Mbeki appointed the Hefer Commission to investigate this claim. If the allegation could not be proved against Ngcuka, the matter would be put to rest there and then. Clearly, unproven allegations would only be allowed to fester and destroy some and not others.

Interestingly, the president changed the terms of reference of the Hefer Commission twice – effectively precluding it from investigating the Scorpions' abuse of power. Ngcuka was cleared by the commission of the spying allegation, and could move on with his life. Mac, described as 'unrepentant' by Ngcuka's law team – a term once used to describe him by his torturers in prison – now became the victim of a media feeding frenzy seemingly bent on eating him alive.

The NPA has never admitted that Mac had nothing to do with awarding the tenders to Shaik's consortium. Despite the third version of the terms of reference, which limited the investigation to whether or not Ngcuka had been a spy, Judge Joos Hefer found that not only were the NPA leaks to the *Sunday Times* an abuse of power, but also that the public opprobrium into which Mac and I had been catapulted as a result of this abuse was 'intolerable' and 'unacceptable'. Yet the allegations of bribery and corruption have been left hanging like a dark cloud over us.

In his own words, this is what former Judge of Appeal and Acting Chief Justice Joos Hefer said:

> It must be … accepted that someone in Mr Ngcuka's office has disclosed information relating to a pending investigation to the press and that this is likely to have occurred contrary to provisions of section 41(6)(a) of the NPA Act … I find Mr Maharaj's evidence most disturbing. As I have already said, it is beyond doubt that leaks did occur. I have also indicated that it is highly likely that the guilty party was within Mr Ngcuka's office and we have it from Mr Ngcuka that he or she could not be traced. Such a state of affairs cannot be tolerated. Months have elapsed since Mr Maharaj was questioned by members of the Investigating Directorate and, although Mr Ngcuka has assured me that the investigation has not been completed, no charges have been preferred against Mr Maharaj or against his wife. In the meantime, press reports about the allegations against them kept appearing. In

a country such as ours where human dignity is a basic constitutional value and every person is presumed to be innocent until he or she is found guilty, this is wholly unacceptable. Section 41(6)(a) of the Prosecuting Authority Act was not enacted for nothing and as long as someone in the National Director's Office keeps flouting the prohibition against the disclosure of information, one cannot be assured that the Prosecuting Authority is being used for the purpose for which it was intended.

These comments by Judge Hefer ostensibly led the Presidency to set up an inquiry into the leaks made by the Scorpions. However, if this ever took place, we were never informed of its findings.

Yet the 'investigations continue' with regard to Mac, presumably because they must find at least something with which to charge us or lose face, having tainted us with such devastating corruption allegations. I recalled the words in Mac's goodbye letter: 'How it pains me that we – the makers of revolution, which is about humanity – are ourselves becoming unfeeling.'

So where did that leave our family?

In June 2003, when First Rand Bank, concerned about its bottom line, became nervous of the intensifying political offensive against Mac, he did the honourable thing and resigned. I too quit my job in 2003. Our salaries dried up. Potential employers became too afraid for their businesses to be seen to be supporting us.

'Is this the freedom we fought for?' Milou asked one day in exasperation.

'You said the enemy's assaults on our well-being would eventually end now that they were becoming a spent force,' Joey lamented. 'You never said the sights of some of our own comrades would become trained on us!'

Milou reminded Joey of the fracas outside South Africa House when Vula was disowned as an ANC initiative in the full glare of the TV news cameras. Now he tried to tell her that these new developments were just a continuation of the same kind of denial of Mac's commitment and integrity by a few in power.

'Now that he's retired from politics, why don't they just leave him alone? It's not as if he's a political threat to anyone,' Joey said, deeply upset.

The threat to 'bring Mac down', executed in the new South Africa with an animosity we could not have imagined would run so deep, not only tarnished Mac's reputation and our name, it undermined our very livelihood.

Early in 1995, Milou had begun to show signs of a nervous breakdown. By the following year, he was in therapy. According to the professionals, his 'deep emotional trauma' was the inevitable result of what, by any standards, had been a disturbed childhood. It did not help, they said, that he was incredibly bright and perceptive. But with the excellent treatment he was receiving, he slowly started recovering.

I had a long chat with Oprah Winfrey over breakfast on Christmas Eve 2002 at Shambala Lodge, where Madiba was hosting a few of his friends. Afterwards, she wrote to me about Milou's condition. This is what she said in the e-mail:

> Yours is a situation where the whole family should be in therapy. Whatever is going on is not just your son's issues. The entire family has been traumatized and he is acting it out … Years ago I did a show called 'Black Sheep of the Family' … and the psychologist on that show said a most memorable thing … that there's no such thing as a black sheep, that the child who's perceived as the black sheep is usually the most sensitive one in the family who 'feels' all the emotions the rest of the family hides, represses, denies. That all families carry their own energy and the most sensitive child absorbs all the energy from everybody. And that the 'black sheep' is usually also the smartest sheep.

Her words confirmed for me that the struggle had exacted its toll on our family, and that by repressing our feelings we had contributed towards Milou's nervous collapse. And now, as he was beginning to recover, a total onslaught on our newfound stability in the form of agonising injustices – inflicted against us by some of the very people with whom we had shared the trenches of struggle – contributed to impairing his recovery.

Like his sister, Milou was shocked by the 'go-for-their-jugular' ferocity with which we were set upon. Yet what we had wanted – and expected – most of all after liberation was some space in which to heal and move on with our lives. That was why Mac served only one term in government.

Like so many children of the struggle, Milou and Joey's real prize as they became young adults was deep pride in our contribution as a family to the process of creating a free and democratic South Africa. Now they were begrudged even the enjoyment of this prize. How deeply ironic that they had to suffer the most chilling blows to our family *after* freedom had been gained, when they thought their days as young foot soldiers were over. How deeply ironic that we have not been allowed to live peacefully in the house we helped build.

A friend from abroad, disturbed by our plight, wrote to Mac recently, three years after the *Sunday Times* article first appeared:

You have spent most of your life in physical danger, your very life itself under permanent threat … But you were fortified by the strong conviction of the justness of your cause, by the camaraderie of the ANC. And by the defined role you had within the struggle. You had a clear purpose and with it a clear sense of who you were. Then came victory and, finally, public awareness and public acknowledgement of the part you played in it, of your bravery and sacrifice.

And in peace – still an heroic role. Negotiation, reconstruction, a ministerial portfolio. Then retirement. And then the rumours begin. No longer threats to your physical person (though that might have been/be there, I don't know) but this time threats to something you value far more highly: your integrity and your sense of your self. The two things that have sustained you through the decades of danger now under attack. An ill-defined threat that won't materialize and yet won't go away; shadowy, nothing that can be fought, dogging your every move. You no longer have an external cause; you are no longer part of a group bound by ideology and close-knit danger. You are operating on your own and perhaps you do not always know who to count on. This is a new war zone ...

Indeed, we are in a new war zone. As recently as 26 March 2006, the *Sunday Times* published a new, false claim that Mac had received R280 000.00 of the late Brett Kebble's 'dirty millions'. This claim is justified on the basis of a list Kebble is supposed to have made of those he lent money to, and which was apparently found on his desk after his death in September 2005. Mac was never given a cent by Kebble, not as a loan or for any other reason. He was merely acquainted with the man! Yet Mac's name is at the top of the list in the *Sunday Times* report of those who are alleged to have benefited from Kebble's largesse. Overseas at the time of this report, Mac became aware of the article for the first time only after it was published. The campaign to smear our name clearly persists unashamedly.

Mac is not free to get on with his life. Our family is still denied the fully liveable lives all South Africans deserve. We continue in the struggle for justice.

Yet what a wonderful and fulfilling life it has been despite these problems. Being part of a successful freedom struggle does not immunise one against pain. Nor does it guarantee personal security and tranquillity. Yet, for all the setbacks, our children are growing up in a free South Africa. They, like our country, are not unmarred by the traumas of the past. But they, like all our countrywomen and countrymen, do not have to face imprisonment, torture, exile and death to achieve the simple joys that life has to offer.

Mac and I take pride in the choices we have made and the endeavours we undertook to help make the new South Africa, with all its problems, a reality for millions, with the promise of a better life for generations to come.

Index

Do you have any comments, suggestions or feedback about this book or any other Zebra Press titles? Contact us at **talkback@zebrapress.co.za**